A Feminist Approach to Sensitive Research

I0123777

This book explores the development and implementation of the Clay Embodiment Research Method (CERM) with one of the most stigmatized, oppressed, and marginalized groups of women in Nepal: sex-trafficked women.

It argues for the use of a feminist approach to such research given the prevailing patriarchal norms, cultural sensitivity of reproductive health, stigmatization of sex trafficking, and low literacy of the women involved. Beginning with an exploration of the author's relationship with Nepal and the women who guide the study, and the realization that a more accessible research approach was needed than the techniques otherwise commonly used, it discusses the use of clay and photography as ideal entry points to engaging with the women in the research and creating this ethical methodology for self-empowerment. Not only does the volume highlight extraordinary insights offered by the women involved in this study through the application of CERM, but also the recognition that its use requires expertise that can deal with the potential elicitation of trauma. The book makes the case for further study on improving the method's use in research, education, and therapy involving low-literate, stigmatized, oppressed, and marginalized populations, particularly where cultural sensitivity is an important consideration.

A Feminist Approach to Sensitive Research is suitable for students, scholars, and researchers in Gender Studies, Sociology, Health Studies, Anthropology, and Asian Studies.

Dr. Tricia Ong is Lecturer in Career Education and a member of the Deakin Research for Violence Against Women hub at Deakin University, Melbourne, Australia. This is her first book. She has published on the multiplicity of stigma of sex-trafficked women in Nepal, clay as a medium in three-dimensional body-mapping, and on the impact of patriarchal norms on young, sex-trafficked women in Nepal. She has also written non-academic articles on women's reproductive health issues.

Focus on Global Gender and Sexuality

www.routledge.com/Focus-on-Global-Gender-and-Sexuality/book-series/FGGS

A Feminist Approach to Sensitive Research

Designing the Clay Embodiment Research Method

Tricia Ong

Routledge
Taylor & Francis Group

LONDON AND NEW YORK

First published 2023
by Routledge
4 Park Square, Milton Park, Abingdon, Oxon OX14 4RN

and by Routledge
605 Third Avenue, New York, NY 10158

Routledge is an imprint of the Taylor & Francis Group, an informa business

© 2023 Tricia Ong

British Library Cataloguing-in-Publication Data
A catalogue record for this book is available from the British Library

Library of Congress Cataloging-in-Publication Data
Names: Ong, Tricia, author.
Title: A feminist approach to sensitive research: designing the clay embodiment research method / Tricia Ong.
Description: Milton Park, Abingdon, Oxon; New York, NY: Routledge, 2023. |
Series: Focus on global gender and sexuality |
Includes bibliographical references and index. |
Identifiers: LCCN 2022031819 (print) | LCCN 2022031820 (ebook) |
Subjects: LCSH: Feminism–Research–Nepal. | Feminism–Study and teaching–Nepal. | Human trafficking–Nepal.
Classification: LCC HQ1181.N35 O54 2023 (print) |
LCC HQ1181.N35 (ebook) | DDC 305.4072/095496–dc23/eng/20220818
LC record available at https://lccn.loc.gov/2022031819
LC ebook record available at https://lccn.loc.gov/2022031820

ISBN: 978-1-032-25724-2 (hbk)
ISBN: 978-1-032-40565-0 (pbk)
ISBN: 978-1-003-35365-2 (ebk)

DOI: 10.4324/b23275

Typeset in Times New Roman
by Newgen Publishing UK

To Smriti Khadka, staff and the women and girls of Asha Nepal. This book was always meant for you and we hope that it can bring 'asha' (hope) to the lives of many women and girls in your care.

Contents

Preface

In March 2011, I embarked on a work journey to Nepal that would change the course of my life. From catching glimpses of the Himalayas, staying in a guesthouse on the grounds of the Shechan Tennyi Dargyeling Monastery in Boudhanath, to running art therapy and women's reproductive health sessions with sex-trafficked Nepalese women and girls, it was a profoundly moving experience. For all too short a time, I was in the company of a generous collective of people living lives that so contrasted my own. On the rooftop of a guesthouse in a town that fills its air with smoke from firing clay into bricks, the amazing Smriti Khadka described the work of Asha Nepal, a Nepalese non-government organization she manages, which shelters and helps rehabilitate sex-trafficked women and girls into the community of Kathmandu and teaches life skills to enable them to build a life with dignity beyond sex trafficking and, in some cases, return home to their families. While in Nepal, I found myself reflecting on my work, life, motherhood and protecting my own daughter, who was the same age of many of the trafficked girls I worked with there (see Ong 2011).

Just days before leaving Nepal, I was given the inspiration to return. As I said goodbye to everyone at Asha Nepal, a young, trafficked girl I had just met looked me in the eye and said, in English: "Don't forget us". I felt a tacit thread being woven between her heart and mine. On my last night, I watched Kutumba, Nepal's most popular folk band, perform the trekking song "Ray Sum Fee Riri" on the steps of the Shechan Monastery at dusk. It took me back 24 years to when, as a 21-year-old, I first trekked the Himalayan mountains, and the awe of my first trip to Nepal trip came flooding back.

I returned to Australia unsettled by my experience in Nepal. It felt "incomplete", and I longed to return. Powerful reminders kept my mind on the Nepalese women I had met, including a viewing of the documentary *The Day My God Died* (2003) on one of Nepal's sex-trafficking pathways – trafficking to India – which featured Anuradha Koirala, the founder and the director of Maiti Nepal, a Nepal-based non-profit organization supporting sex-trafficked women. This was followed by a deeply moving conversation with Anuradha at a subsequent fundraising dinner when she was in Australia to promote the work of Maiti Nepal. I then got to know the Nepalese diaspora community in Melbourne, Australia, and their open-hearted conversations and celebrations helped me navigate Nepalese culture.

Several months later, I was back in Nepal, arriving in the middle of the (Hindu) Dashain Festival, a festival honoured by all of Nepal's 100 ethnic groups regardless of the religion they practise. From friendships formed in my earlier visit, I stayed with Hindu and Buddhist families in Kathmandu. I received family *tikka* (blessings) on the tenth (Blessing) Day of the Dashain Festival. I trekked in the Annapurna region with Nepalese friends and saw the magnificent Machapuchare (fishtail) mountain, which holds iconic memories of Nepal for me. I partook in rituals of the (Hindu) Tihar Festival or "Festival of Lights". I visited Maiti Nepal and women I had worked with on my earlier trip. I visited Smriti at Asha Nepal.

Yet, I left Nepal with the same sense of longing to be back as before. A year later, I returned, this time for a Hindu Newari wedding at which I was given a red sāri by the family for their daughter's wedding. It was the (Hindu) month of Mangsir, an auspicious month to get married in Nepalese society, and I observed not one but many weddings at Hindu temples and in family homes. I became very engrossed in the varied traditional practices of Nepal's many different ethnic groups and their impact on Nepalese women and being right at the doorstep to Nepal's caste system. I later contributed an article to *Pipalbot*, a Nepalese community newspaper in Melbourne, about weddings in Nepal (Ong 2013a) and, after, I attended a Teej Hindu women's festival celebrated to honour the union of Lord Shiva and Goddess Parbati in which I wore my red sāri, which attracted the most comments from Nepalese readers (Ong 2013b).

On my last day of the wedding journey, I visited Smriti at Asha Nepal. We cofacilitated a reproductive health workshop together with adolescent girls at Asha Nepal, which gave me further insights into reproductive health issues for Nepalese women and girls. I learned further rudimentary Nepali. Over *masala chia* (Nepali spiced tea), we had a long discussion about adolescent girls and reproductive health in Nepal and a reproductive health training manual she was developing for the adolescent girls at Asha Nepal. At the end of our conversation, she took my hands, looked into my eyes, and said, "I really want to work with you". I returned her gaze and said, "Let's make it happen. I promise I will find a way".

References

Ong, T. 2011. Returning to Nepal: a creative arts therapy experience. *Returningtonepal.* https://returningtonepal.wordpress.com/ [Accessed 17 March 2022].

Ong, T. 2013a. Mangsir, a truly special wedding month. *Pipalbot.* https://issuu.com/pipalbot/docs/pipalbot_130313/12 [Accessed 17 March 2022].

Ong, T. 2013b. The Teej Festival: an ancient Hindu tradition for women in changing times. *Pipalbot.* https://issuu.com/pipalbot/docs/pipalbot_16_sept/14 [Accessed 17 March 2022].

The Day My God Died. 2003. *Directed by Andrew Levine.* Canada: Andrew Levine Productions.

Acknowledgements

It was a personal goal to pen a book on my experiences in Nepal after I completed my Doctor of Philosophy (PhD) degree in 2018. However, it was unexpected to see it being moulded through clay. But it was – when it happened – an unexpected joy.

Thank you to the staff of the School of Health and Development, members of the Deakin Research on Violence Against Women hub, and my colleagues at DeakinTALENT – Graduate Employment Division – at Deakin University, for the encouragement to write in and among Covid-19 lockdowns in Melbourne, Australia, and through the flux of work uncertainties.

Thank you also to Francis Ong, who walked my PhD journey with me and helped me to sculpt this book into its final shape. I cannot thank you enough.

Tables

Figures

Acronyms

AIDS	acquired immunodeficiency syndrome
ARSH	adolescent sexual and reproductive health
BYIF	Bhaktapur Youth Information Forum
CAP Nepal	Centre for Awareness and Promotion Nepal
CCAS	Community Children's Art Centre
CERM	Clay Embodiment Research Method
CSE	comprehensive sexuality education
DUHREC	Deakin University's Human Research Ethics Committee
FPAN	Family Planning Association of Nepal
HIV	human immunodeficiency virus
IVF	in vitro fertilization
NGOs	non-government organizations
NHRC	Nepal Health Research Council
PAR	participatory action research
PCOS	polycystic ovary syndrome
SEE	Skills, Education and Empowerment
STD	sexually transmitted disease
UNFPA	United Nations Population Fund
Y-PEER Nepal	Youth-Peer Nepal

1 Introduction

Being "invited in"

About this book

This book describes a path to authentically engage with low-literate, stigmatized, oppressed, and marginalized women to elicit their reproductive health knowledge, specifically perceptions of reproductive functioning, in biological, health, and societal contexts. The authenticity here refers to reaching past cultural proprieties, patriarchy, and non-verbal traditions of communicating, to give voice to experiences despite shame, humiliation, taboos, acceptance of stigma, and cultural suppression of doing so.

The people who are the focus of this book are, first and foremost, young women and girls of Nepal who, in addition to living in a heavily patriarchal society, are burdened with severe economic, social, and psychological hardships, as a consequence of their experience of sex trafficking in Nepal. Then there are those who have impacted the women's experience of life, notably their parents, husbands, and other Nepalese men. There are also the international non-government organizations, non-government organizations (NGOs), and other local Nepalese agencies that help to support them to live the lives of their choosing.

The book's general aim is to describe a methodology – the Clay Embodiment Research Method (CERM) – and its foundations, so that its appropriate use can be assessed and provide researchers, educators, and therapists an insight into designing a research method for sensitive research with vulnerable populations in other cultures. The methodology has, I believe, evidently wide application across research, education, and therapeutic settings, and especially so in those where "Western" or established verbal approaches are severely hampered by cultural sensitivities and/or people's different ways of knowing. Moreover, the methodology is open to adaptation according to the needs of the practitioner.

DOI: 10.4324/b23275-1

This necessitates a description of its developmental journey and its effect on people to whom it was developed for (our research participants) and on those who apply it (the researchers). The description here is set in the context of stigmatized, oppressed, and marginalized women in Nepal. The setting is broad enough to provide opportunity to envision how the methodology described could be used, or adapted for use, in other settings, while allowing the depth necessary to closely examine challenges faced and the effects of the use of the methodology.

The Nepali context – a personal journey

In late 2010, I was invited to work on an art therapy and women's reproductive health project with sex-trafficked women in Nepal with Art2Healing, an Australian not-for-profit organization (see Art2Healing 2017). The work I did there led to realizations that profoundly shaped work I did afterwards. Then, I was working as a creative arts therapist in the women's reproductive health field in Melbourne, Australia, including with women with endometriosis, ovarian cancer, polycystic ovary syndrome (PCOS), and women undergoing in vitro fertilization (IVF). The experience of working with sex-trafficked women living in extreme impoverishment and hardship in a heavily patriarchal society comprising 100 ethnicities embedding cultural practices that, through an outsider's eyes, are remarkable, led me to realizations that there were important problems here that I could potentially help address. In so doing, this would be deeply meaningful to me given my quickly growing interest in the women and their issues and my observations of the some of the efforts of organizations and well-meaning individuals doing work there that I could see had little actual benefit for Nepalese women and, in some cases, caused harm.

It took a few years for me to figure out what I could do. I had returned to Nepal a few times, drawn back by the people I had met, met more, and tried to better understand the culture I was generously invited into. I recalled working with Smriti Khadka, manager of Asha Nepal, a UK charity and Nepalese NGO in Nepal that works with sexually abused and sex-trafficked girls (Asha Nepal 2021), cofacilitating a reproductive health workshop for adolescent girls with her in Kathmandu, and later helping her to develop an adolescent girls' reproductive health training manual (from Australia) and pilot of a reproductive health education training programme she hoped to implement at Asha Nepal. Meanwhile, in Australia, I grew friendships within the large Nepalese community, taking part in community festivals and contributing to *Pipalbot*, their community newspaper. I wrote of my insights from work in Nepal in a research journal (see Ong 2013) and kept researching the Nepalese reproductive health and sex-trafficking context.

In 2014, the ongoing engagement with Nepal and self-reflection produced a research topic that formed the basis of my Doctor of Philosophy (PhD) degree at Deakin University, Australia. In essence, what I set out to do was to explore the reproductive health knowledge of young women who had been trafficked into the sex industry in Nepal, so as to develop recommendations for reproductive health education and reproductive health support for them. I knew from my earlier work facilitating clay workshops in Nepal with Art2Healing that clay was a medium that can release thoughts that Nepalese sex-trafficked women girls otherwise keep submerged in their unconsciousness and even from each other. My proposal – the Clay Embodiment Research Method (CERM) – was a structured process built around the use of clay and photography, and draws on insights from earlier workshops in Nepal, creative arts therapy practice and tools, and from relevant feminist theories and research methods.

To better appreciate the research difficulties this methodology helps overcome – namely, cultural sensitivities and educational constraints – we need to understand the societal mindset of our research subjects. In my case, it is that of Nepal, its 100 ethnicities, multiple religions, 126 languages, and a diversity of cultures, but a predominantly Hindu society. I discuss Nepal and its culture and the impact on women, especially in sexual and reproductive health contexts, in the next chapter. For now, let me introduce the sex industry in Nepal and the remarkable women from our last, and most comprehensive, application of the methodology and my Nepalese research assistant.

The sex industry in Nepal

In Nepal, the entertainment industry acts as a front for the sex industry (Frederick, Basynet and Aguettant 2010, Caviglia 2018). Its hub is in the capital, Kathmandu. The sex industry operates out of cabin restaurants – crude constructions with private areas separated by plywood or curtains – *bhatti pasals* (wine shops), massage parlours, dance bars, *dohori sanjh* (restaurants where traditional male and female duets are performed), and also guest houses/lodges (Frederick, Basynet and Aguettant 2010). They attract army officers, government officials, police, small businessmen, service holders, internal migrants, and men who made money through overseas labour or real estate (Frederick, Basynet and Aguettant 2010). Their owners are men or former sex workers (Frederick, Basynet and Aguettant 2010, Caviglia 2018).

The sex industry is female-dominated (Subedi 2009). Approximately 50,000 girls work in the industry and their young age (under 18) – girls as young as nine have been found working in the industry (Frederick, Basynet and Aguettant 2010) – is an indicator of trafficking (National Human Rights Commission 2014). For many who conduct sex work, by choice or coercion, rape is accepted as a fact of life (Frederick, Basynet and Aguettant 2010). Although comparative research has not been done, informal observations indicate that "violence against women and girls in Nepal's entertainment industry exceeds that of similar entertainment industries in many parts of the world, including Thailand, Hong Kong, Malaysia, United Arab Emirates, India and Western Europe" (Frederick, Basynet and Aguettant 2010: 49). The main users are married men aged 36 to 50 years (Frederick, Basynet and Aguettant 2010, Caviglia 2018).

Six sex-trafficked women

To better illustrate the use of the CERM in this book, I will draw on the personal stories offered by some of the women who experienced its use as the subjects of our research or as workshop participants, as well as our – the researchers and workshop facilitators – own observations and feelings. To provide continuity of thought and storytelling through the stages of the methodology, we will largely focus on six participants (research subjects) from the field research of my PhD candidature and my research assistant. The women are, first and foremost, young women who had been trafficked into the sex industry in Nepal, but throughout this book – for ease of discussion – we will refer to them as "sex-trafficked women".

For context to what they say and do, we should provide here some pertinent information about each of the women. (Pseudonyms have been used to protect their identities.) We did not ask about their experiences of being trafficked, as it was not pertinent to the purpose of our research, and it was clearly painful. The first four women were sheltered by Asha Nepal, a UK charity and administered NGO in Nepal that cares for and provides training to girls who have been sexually abused and trafficked for sexual exploitation. The other two women were supported, but not housed, by another NGO, the Centre for Awareness and Promotion Nepal (CAP Nepal). All interactions with the women were at Asha Nepal and CAP Nepal's homes.

Niuresha was 17 years old from a Tamang ethnic group in the Nuwachot district. She is Buddhist, was unmarried, and had no children. She was trafficked into hotels and guest houses by unspecified members of her family and rescued after several months. The lingering impact of her experience includes only periodical attendance at school. When I first met her, I was struck by her beauty and poise, and her curiosity for new knowledge.

Rosina was 14 years old, from a Magar ethnic group in the Myagdi district. She is Buddhist, was unmarried, and had no children. She was trafficked into a hotel by her stepfather and rescued approximately a year later. She had been in school only periodically as a lingering consequence. On first meeting, I saw an innocent young girl just stepping into the world. However, as I got to know her, I realized she bore scars from trafficking, manifesting as highly sexualized dancing when Asha Nepal staff were not around, and in the information she revealed in workshops.

Soniya was 18 years old, from a Brahmin ethnic group in the Lalitpur district. She is Hindu, was unmarried, and had no children. She was trafficked into a massage parlour by her sister-in-law and managed to escape after a few weeks. This still had an effect on her school attendance. She was also sexually abused before being trafficked. She gravitated towards me at our first meeting, and she struck me as strong, yet fragile. It later became clear that she was challenging the more harmful aspects of accepted practices of Nepali culture. For example, she escaped from sex trafficking.

Sulob was 18 years old, from a Tamang ethnic group in the Nuwachot district. She is Buddhist, was unmarried, and had no children. She was trafficked into a restaurant by a friend before being rescued some months later. She too had problems in consistently attending school. She seemed rebellious and longed to live in the heart of the city, away from the staid confines of Asha Nepal. She sometimes wore make-up when venturing out that, on the streets of Kathmandu, hinted (falsely) at being a sex worker. I saw her get one of the other girls at Asha Nepal to sew her clothes on so they were skin tight and showed off her slenderness. At first, I thought she might be difficult to work with in our research. However, she was just the opposite.

Aisha was 20 years, from Sanku in the Kathmandu district (although CAP Nepal staff were not sure if she born in this district or migrated there from rural eastern Nepal). She said she was Chettri, though her appearance seemed unlike the general people from that ethnic group. In one of our workshops, we observed that she was uncomfortable discussing this identity. It has been reported that Dalit women and girls working in the sex industry in Nepal often change their names to assume "high caste" identities to avoid discrimination (Frederick, Basnyat and Aguettant 2010). She is Hindu, was married, with one daughter, and had never been to school. She was trafficked into a restaurant then dance bar in Kathmandu by an actor who came to perform in her village. This may have been over a number of years. Aisha came from a troubled home of four girls whose family could not afford to educate them. In addition to the violence of the trafficking, she was subject to sexual violence from her husband's uncle and ongoing intimate partner violence living in a one-room home with her husband. She had an aggressive demeanour when we first met and her baby daughter was fretful and seemed frightened of strangers.

Indira was 22 years old, of a Magar ethnic group in Myagdi district. It was unclear whether she was Hindu or Buddhist, as some Magar communities practice both religions. She was married with an infant son. She completed high school (class 12). She was trafficked into a cabin restaurant then a dance bar, by whom or for how long we did not know. She withdrew from the study for personal reasons after the fifth clay body-mapping workshop. I felt she did not quite trust us (my young Nepalese research assistant and I) as much as the other women and girls.

A young female Nepali perspective of the CERM

I recently asked my research assistant in Nepal, Sabrina Chettri, a curious (then) 25-year-old single, well-educated Nepali woman what she thought of her experience working with clay with the sex-trafficked women. For context, she, like most Nepalis, have an awareness of sex trafficking in their midst. However, she had no direct exposure to it until being the primary interpreter between our research participants and I, and my workshop cofacilitator. She said:

> I vividly remember the day of my interview for research assistant, I had just graduated from my college and was working for the Family Planning Association, where we were basically orienting/conducting awareness programmes for the government school students. Therefore, I really hoped and wished to work on the project proposed by Tricia. Working for the project enlightened me about the reality that was covered from a normal girl like me. I was shocked every single time we sat for a clay session with the girls, shaken by every information provided by the girls. Not only were we gaining their trust but, to be frank, I was learning a lot from them. I always had a superficial/textbook knowledge about the topics that we covered. Like I mentioned, being a normally brought up daughter, sister, and friend, these topics were far from the topic discussed in my home, school or friend circle. I had no idea about

the things shared and also didn't ever feel that it exists in reality except for the newspaper.

I also particularly remember how they were trying to share their real-life experience through the clay, and that we were mesmerized with their art, which was so abstract and captured a lot of memories and emotions that involved sadness, happiness, relief, stress and betrayal etc. I also remember sessions that brought tears to my eyes, with the fact that these girls had to face so much cruelty from society at the age where they were expected not to know anything about the topics covered. I would also like to compare the very first day of the clay session, where they were not very sure about us, with the last session, where they were super sad. Sad for the fact that it was the last day of the session. It was at these sessions that they, after years, were able to open up about the experience. I am pretty sure they had millions of experiences to share with us.

Overall, I can write a whole book about my experience working for the project. (do keep this ;))

I can state that, because of this project, I had an opportunity to learn new things and experience new ways of communication (the Clay Method). I would also like to highlight that the experience collected has helped me in my personal life as well. I am very grateful and thankful that I was able to be a part of the whole journey and the opportunity provided.

Structure of the book

Chapter 2 describes the social and cultural environment in which we used the CERM. It focusses on the cultural sensitivity of sexual and reproductive health for women in Nepal, and sex trafficking, leading to the vulnerability – stigmatization, oppression, and marginalization – of sex-trafficked women. This takes us to Chapter 3 on the rationale of drawing on critical ethnography and inspiration from participatory action research to adopt a feminist approach to methods development, research analysis and writing.

Chapter 4 introduces CERM in two parts: Part 1 describes the discoveries that led to using clay and photography. Part 2 discusses the evolution of the methodology and describes its application with young sex-trafficked women in Nepal.

Chapter 5 discusses the ethical considerations of designing a new research method in a complex cross-cultural context. It describes the marked difference in ethics consideration between our Australian sponsors (Deakin University Human Research Ethics Committee) and that of the Nepal Health Research Council.

Chapter 6 discusses the practicalities of working with clay in Nepal, and the challenges of conducting our research in Nepal generally.

In Chapter 7 we look at the power of CERM in reproductive health research and education, and the risks of using clay and photography, which posits proper training for its use. It points to expertise and local relationships as being essential to the success of the methodology in Nepal.

Chapter 8 provides concluding remarks on the book. This includes commentary on the future use of CERM in reproductive health education in Nepal and beyond, and a "call to action" to further research clay body-mapping, given both their accessibility and risks as a communication medium in research with vulnerable populations.

References

Art2Healing. 2017. About. *Art2Healing.* https://www.arttohealing.org/ [Accessed 9 April 2022].

Asha Nepal. 2021. About. *Asha Nepal.* https://asha-nepal.org/about [Accessed 9 April 2022].

Caviglia, L. 2018. *Sex work in Nepal: the making and unmaking of a category.* London: Routledge.

Frederick, J., Basnyat, M. and Aguettant, L. 2010. *Trafficking and exploitation in the entertainment and sex industries in Nepal: a handbook for decision-makers.* Kathmandu: Terres des hommes Foundation. https://www.tdh.ch/sites/default/files/study_trafficking_tdhl_2010.pdf [Accessed 9 April 2022].

National Human Rights Commission. 2014. *Trafficking in persons especially on women and children in Nepal.* Pulchok: National Human Rights Commission. https://reliefweb.int/report/nepal/trafficking-persons-national-report-2013-2015 [Accessed 18 April 2022].

Ong, T. 2013. Nepal – Three cups of tea: ruminating on the writing in the leaves. *Creative Approaches to Research,* 6(3), 48–56.

Subedi, G. 2009. Trafficking in girls and women in Nepal for commercial sexual exploitation: emerging gaps and concerns. *Pakistan Journal of Women's Studies: Alam-e-Niswan,* 16(1–2), 121–46.

2 The impact of patriarchy on women in Nepal

The vulnerability of sex-trafficked women

Introduction

In research, cultural sensitivity is a key challenge that, in our case involving young Nepalese women who had been trafficked into the sex industry, prompted the development of the CERM for reproductive health research. The CERM approach is adaptable to other contexts (different cultures, populations, preferred materials etc.) where addressing such sensitivity is critical to enabling vulnerable women to participate. As an illustration of the challenge, this chapter explores the cultural sensitivity we faced in our research through the lens of Hinduism as it is practised in Nepal. We look at Hinduism's impact on the sexual and reproductive health of Nepalese women over their reproductive life stages, and how this produces strong cultural stigmatization, oppression, and marginalization of sex-trafficked women.

Contemporary Nepal

Nepal is a landlocked country in south Asia bordered by India to its south, west, and east and China (Tibet) to its north. It has a rugged topography – the Upper Himalaya ranges, where Mount Everest is, comprises 15% of Nepal's land area, and the still formidable Lower Himalaya and "middle hills" occupy another 68% (Ministry of Foreign Affairs 2022). 79% of its population of 29 million live in rural regions (World Bank 2022) and are largely dependent on subsistence farming for their livelihoods (International Fund for Agricultural Development 2022). Nepal is on the United Nations' list of least developed countries (United Nations Conference on Trade and Development 2022). One effect of Nepal's geography, poor infrastructure, and general poverty is that the cultural practices of its rural communities (and hence of much

DOI: 10.4324/b23275-2

of its population) remain largely unchanged, isolated as they are from the progressive ideas of the urban elite.

Nepal defines itself as being "All the Nepali people, with multi-ethnic, multi-lingual, multi-religious, multicultural characteristics and in geographical diversities, and having common aspirations and being united by a bond of allegiance to national independence, territorial integrity, national interest and prosperity of Nepal, collectively constitute the nation" (Nepal Law Commission 2020: 3). However, it is dominated by the culture, language (Nepali) and religion (Hinduism) of the Parbatiya (or Pahari) – the "hill people" – a collective of peoples (mainly Chettri or Chhetri, and Brahmin or Bahun) that migrated from the west and south (i.e., from India) (Pradhan 2011). Over time they achieved political union with, and rule over, the peoples that migrated from the east (ethnic groups speaking Tibeto-Burman languages) and those of the Kathmandu Valley, mainly the Newars (Pradhan 2005). The form of Hinduism they practised led to Nepal's society becoming "heavily patriarchal" (Hamal Gurung 2014: 175) but, more fundamentally, it is "the source of the caste system" in Nepal (Schroeder 2004: 717). Caste still matters in Nepalese society today (Brown 1996, Schroeder 2004, Pradhan 2011) and women and girls "face discrimination on multiple levels by virtue of their sex, caste and ethnicity" (Posner et al. 2009: 284). Until 2006, Nepal was the last remaining Hindu kingdom in the world (Schroeder 2004).

Hinduism and caste in Nepal

The person considered most responsible for the influence of Hinduism in Nepalese culture is Jang Bahadur Rana (1817–77), of Chettri ethnicity. Rana proclaimed himself prime minister for life and was the virtual ruler of Nepal from 1846 to 1877, notwithstanding the existence alongside of a monarchy. He established a powerful dynasty of hereditary prime ministers whose grip on Nepal is known colloquially as the Rana Rule (1846–1951). Critically for Nepali culture, he developed the first set of kingdom-wide codified and written law – the Muluki Ain of 1854 (MA of 1854) – one effect of which was to embed Hinduism and its patriarchal norms into Nepalese society. It remained the principal law of the land, largely unchanged, until 1951 when the Rana Rule was overthrown.

The MA of 1854 is a complex document with roots in the Laws of Manu (also known as the Manusmriti or Manav Dharam Shastra), perhaps the most important and authoritative of the Dharmashastra text of Hindu law (Doniger 1991, Milner 1994). The MA of 1854 preserves

Table 2.1 Simplified scheme of the Hindu caste system

Brahmin or Bahun (Nepali)	Highest of the castes, historically having the roles of priests and teachers of sacred knowledge (*veda*)
Kshatriya or Chettri (Nepali)	Second highest caste, historically having the roles of rulers and warriors (protectors of the dominion)
Vaisya	Third highest caste, historically having the roles of farmers (*vish* – "those settled on soils") and merchants
Sudra	Lowest of the castes, historically having the role of providing service to the other castes, including those of labourers and artisans
Dalit or Acchoot (Nepali)	Considered "untouchables" by virtue of their occupations deemed as ritually polluting, notably killing animals, dealing with the dead, and cleaning human waste

Table 2.2 Hindu-centric social stratification (caste) by the Muluki Ain of 1854

Highest ranked: Wearers of the holy thread (*tagadhari*) – Brahmin, Chhetri, and the high castes of other Hindu groups

Second ranked: Non-enslavable alcohol-drinkers (*namasine matwali*) – non-Hindu groups considered indigenous to where they live and that were powerful at the time of the MA of 1854

Third ranked: Enslavable alcohol-drinkers (*masine matwali*) – other non-Hindu indigenous groups

Fourth ranked: Impure but touchable groups (*paninacalne choi chito halnunaparne*) i.e., from whom water could not be accepted but whose contact does not require purification by aspergation of water – groups at the lowest end of the Newar caste system (Hindu), Muslims (*Mussalman*), and Europeans (*Mlecch*)

Fifth ranked: Untouchables (*paninacalne choi chito halnuparne*) i.e., from whom water could not be accepted and whose contact requires purification by aspergation of water – Acchoot/Dalit groups (Hindu)

the Hindu (Parbatiya) caste system (see Table 2.1) while also incorporating the customary laws of the different ethnic groups. It proclaims: "This law has been made in the light of the scriptures [*shastras*], tenets of moral conduct (*niti*), and the experience of the people [*lokko anuhbhav*]" (Pradhan 2005: 10) (see Table 2.2). It was designed to create order in the (abstract) cosmos through imposing a moral, social, and legal code (Sharma 2003 cited in Höfer 2004). The MA of 1854 is unique in that there is no other example of caste validation given to a legal document anywhere else in south Asia (Sharma cited in Höfer 2004: xvi). It determined inter-community relations, the touchability and untouchability of people, purity and impurity rituals (e.g., who can take water and rice from whom), sexual relations, temporal-personal impurity (related to menstruation, childbirth, and mourning), division of labour in the hierarchy, mobility within the hierarchy, and the role of the state (Nepal) vis-à-vis India (Höfer 2004). More than a third of the document deals with sexual relations within and outside of caste groups (Höfer 2004).

Generally speaking, under the MA of 1854 the higher ranked groups (Table 2.2) held the majority of its privileges and the lower ranked groups bore most of its obligations (Geiser 2005). Notwithstanding subsequent efforts at change, its legacy is that, today, caste in Nepal remains a complex, hierarchical, social stratification based on the Hindu concern with ritual purity, that powerfully affects people's everyday lives (Cameron 1998, Grossman-Thompson 2017, Baumann et al. 2021a).

Caste, established at birth, determines status and social responsibilities (Baumann et al. 2021a). Discrimination based on caste and untouchability was first prohibited under Nepal's 1990 Constitution, created following widespread pro-democracy protest and anti-regime unrest, and remains so under the current Constitution (see Nepal Law Commission 2020). Some 20 years after that ground-breaking step, Nepal's Constituent Assembly enacted comprehensive legislation criminalizing caste-based discrimination through the 2011 Caste-Based Discrimination and Untouchability (Offence and Punishment) Act, 2068 "in any public or private place" (Nepal Law Commission 2011: 4). Yet, important as the anti-discrimination legal framework is, caste discrimination remains a reality in Nepal. A 2018 United Nations Nepal survey of 4,000 randomly selected households (across castes) in rural provinces found that nearly all believed that harmful caste discrimination occurred in their community (United Nations Nepal 2020). Since caste is integral to their cultural practices, caste-based discrimination affects nearly all aspects of life – the food people can eat, the communal water sources/taps people can use, the temples, communal spaces and homes/ kitchens people can enter, who can marry whom and the occupations people can have. The issue seems to be one of community rather than political, as the survey found that access to government services is reported as not being a significant problem in the context of caste.

Patriarchy in Nepal

In Nepal, the system of government is controlled by men, its society is focussed and centred on the father and male lineage. The patriarchal system contributes to gender inequalities at many levels of Nepalese society, including in land and resource distribution and the social, economic, and political relations at household and societal levels (Hamal Gurung 2014, De Schutter 2021). The inequalities are large enough to show up in large-scale data sets (census, economic reporting etc.). In these, aspects of patriarchy itself can be glimpsed. For example, the preferential treatment of males in households is discernible in government data: there are more male children (0–9 years male–female sex ratio of 115), and fewer males missed out on school (18% compared to 35% of females) (Central Bureau of Statistics 2019).

As with the caste system, and intimately tied to it, patriarchal norms granting privileges and opportunities to boys and men, and placing obligations and constraints on girls and women, were strongly entrenched across the then Kingdom of Nepal through the MA of 1854 (Grossman-Thompson 2016). As a fundamental component of culture, patriarchy has an inter-generational dimension: "As a daughter, she should be under the surveillance of her father; as a wife, of her husband; and as a widow, of her son" (Mittra and Kumar 2004: 2–3).

The issue of patriarchy, though, is complex. The roles played by men and women vary between and within different communities, according to class, caste, ethnicity, education, religion, age, and marital status. Some suggest that Nepal is a society of "multiple patriarchies" (Tamang 2011: 281). Although gender roles and relations vary, it is the uneducated, rural, and impoverished women that suffer most, living in strongly patriarchal households and society (Hennink and Simkhada 2004, Kaufman and Crawford 2011, Hamal Gurung 2014). Their access to knowledge, skills, resources and opportunities is extremely low (Hennink and Simkhada 2004). In rural areas, women are expected to play the subordinate, submissive, and more conservative gender role in marital relationships (Lamichhane et al. 2011).

High caste women also receive the caste and class privileges of their father and husbands and themselves reinforce patriarchal norms and the caste system generally (Höfer 2004), including the oppression of Dalit women, which is a subject that is not meaningfully acknowledged in "accounts of 'the Nepali woman's' 'oppression' by 'women leaders'" (Tamang 2011: 286). However, while women are often framed as inferior, many of them do not subscribe to the caste system (Cameron 1998).

The impact on Hinduism and its patriarchal norms on the sexual and reproductive health of Nepali women

Hinduism in Nepal demands that a female is raised from birth to death to be dependent on, and be subservient to, men (Samarasinghe 2008:

64). Patriarchy begins at home and is present throughout her life. Its most impactful time is her reproductive life years – at menstruation, marriage, and in relation to sexual intercourse.

Menarche and menstruation

In Hinduism, bodily secretions, such as faeces, urine, blood, fat, marrow, nails (cuttings), mucus, sweat, etc., are seen as polluting (Höfer 2004). As such, women are deemed to be impure at menstruation – from menarche to menopause (Kondos 2004) – regardless of caste (Standing and Parker 2017). Birth is also perceived as 'polluting' in Nepali culture and post-partum women are deemed impure (Höfer 2004, Posner et al. 2009, Sharma et al. 2016, Kaphle 2021). Menstrual pollution beliefs are widespread (Cameron 1998, Bennett 2002, Crawford, Menger and Kaufman 2014) particularly in remote rural regions (Adhikari et al. 2007, Sapkota et al. 2013, Standing and Parker 2017, Baumann, Lhaki and Burke 2019, Ong, Mellor and Chettri 2019, Baumann et al. 2021a). Hindu beliefs on menstruation have also suppressed the belief systems of some Buddhist communities (Bhartiya 2013) who consider menstruation to be a natural and normal physiological process (Ranabhat et al. 2015, Ong, Mellor and Chettri 2019). As with other Hindu beliefs, their place in Nepali culture can be traced to the MA of 1854. For example, it specifies that a "place" becomes impure if a woman who is menstruating enters it (Höfer 2004).

Ritualistic purity is a basic tenet in Hinduism. The Hindu "solution" to the impurity wrought is for the menstruating or post-partum woman to be isolated so as not to contaminate others and, in the latter case, subsequently ritually cleansed (Höfer 2004, Sharma et al. 2016). A menstruating woman cannot share a bed with her husband, nor enter a kitchen, let alone prepare food. She cannot touch a male person even if he is a relative (Crawford, Menger and Kaufman 2014, Baumann, Lhaki and Burke 2019, Ong, Mellor and Chettri 2019) nor look in the direction of her father's house (Kondos 2004, Ong, Mellor and Chettri 2019). She cannot participate in social or religious activities including worshipping in temples (Sapkota et al. 2013, Baumann, Lhaki and Burke 2019, Ong, Mellor and Chettri 2019) and in the lighting of holy lamps (Archarya, Shakya and Sthapit 2011). Depending on the community she is in, the menstruating women may be obliged to refrain from using public taps or from looking at her reflection (Mahon and Fernandes 2010, Baumann, Lhaki and Burke 2019). She may be forbidden certain chores (Sapkota et al. 2013) or required to bathe only with cold water (Ong, Mellor and Chettri 2019), or cannot bathe at all (Baumann, Lhaki and Burke 2019).

In some Hindu communities, menarche is marked with the custom of *gupha basne* (literally "staying in a cave") wherein the young girl stays basically alone in a darkened room for up to 12 days (Bennett 1976, Crawford, Menger and Kaufman 2014). Prior to puberty, some Hindu families give *guniyo cholo* to their daughters (Narayna and Purkayastha 2009, Ong, Mellor and Chettri 2019). *Guniyo* means sāri and *cholo* means blouse (Kondos 2004). The term comes from a Hindu concept that roughly translates to the qualities that determine a person and is marked by a "coming of age" ritual for girls in some communities Nepal with a religious *tikka* (blessing) ceremony and gift of a sāri and blouse (Kondos 2004, Ong, Mellor and Chettri 2019). However, in a similar Parbatiya tradition (not called *guniyo cholo*), women are given a new red sāri after seclusion at menarche: presented by fathers signifying a girl's transformation to womanhood and her marriageability (Kondos 2004). This contrasts with other coming of age (at menarche) traditions in Nepal, which do not have marriage implications.

In the harshest Hindu menstruation traditions, women and girls are sent to a *goth* (house) in a practice known as *chaupadi* (or *chhaupadi*)[1]. *Chhau* is defined as "untouchable, unclean or impure" and *padi* refers to "being or becoming" (Nepal Fertility Care Centre 2015 cited in Baumann et al. 2021a, United Nations Populations Fund, United Nations Children's Fund and United Nations Volunteers 2020). Broadly speaking, *chhaupadi* refers to the state of being untouchable or unclean (Bist 2014, Baumann et al. 2021a) and is a belief from Hindu religious mythology (Cameron 1998, Baumann et al. 2021a).

The practice contributes to reproductive health problems arising from poor hygiene practices and unsanitary conditions (Ranabhat et al. 2015, Standing and Parker 2017). As recently as 2019, women and children have died because of smoke inhalation in the poorly ventilated (single small window) *chaupadi* huts (see Sharma and Schultz 2019). While isolated in *chaupadi*, women in the far western districts have experienced rape and physical assault (Dahal 2008, Yadav et al. 2017), including by their husbands (Cardoso et al. 2019). The practice of *chaupadi* was outlawed in Nepal in 2005 (Robinson 2015) but, from survey data, is still clearly practised in rural districts (UN Nepal 2020) despite the prospect of fines and jail time in 2017 (Baumann et al. 2021b). There have been government efforts to remove *chaupadi* huts in the remote far western districts where the practice appears entrenched despite education (Adhikari 2020). However, the communities sometimes rebuild the huts. Even in districts where *chaupadi* huts are no longer used, the practice of seclusion persists in the form of the women going to another house by themselves or to a room in their house (Yadav et al. 2017, Ong 2018, Ong, Mellor and Chettri 2019), though sometimes mother and sisters sit with secluded women at night (Ong 2018). In Nepal, menstruation is also a major life stressor that keeps girls out of school often for extended periods of time (Yilmaz, Bohara and Thapa 2021). Yet 44% of women surveyed by Baumann, Lhaki and Burke (2019) see it as a positive aspect of life. Local community and household menstrual practices vary broadly according to ethnic group and caste, and more specifically determined by religious and spiritual beliefs, family traditions, the appreciation of negative consequences, the level of formal education and social pressure (Posner et al. 2009, Baumann, Lhaki and Burke 2019, Ong, Mellor and Chettri 2019, Mukherjee et al. 2020). Broadly speaking, Brahmin/Chhetri (high caste) women have better knowledge of what menstruation is, and better sanitary practices, than other ethnicities/castes. Interestingly, Dalits appear to have the most positive attitude to menstruation (Baumann, Lhaki and Burke 2019). Looking more specifically at women in the Kathmandu Valley (i.e., more urbanized and better educated women), Mukherjee et al. (2020) found them more willing to ignore customary avoidance of social gatherings yet remain attentive to avoiding religious ones, perhaps because the religious dimension (impurity/untouchable) is deeply internalized. Their study on menstruation restriction practices suggested that "educated and urban women are still victims of guilt, insecurity and humiliation" (Mukherjee et al. 2020: 8).

Early marriage and early childbearing

It is a Nepali cultural expectation for women to marry (Frederick 2000, Crawford and Kaufman 2008, Hamal Gurung 2014), and girls are socialized to believe that marriage is the ultimate goal in their lives (Samarasinghe 2008). Ancient Hindu texts state that marriage should not be delayed until much after puberty (Mittra and Kumar 2004). Although Nepal's National Civil Code Act 2017 defines the legal age for marriage as 20 years for men and women (Batyra and Pesendo 2021), and child marriage has been outlawed since 1963 (Shahi et al. 2019), adolescent marriage is viewed to be the norm in many ethnic groups (Puri, Shah and Tamang 2010, Puri, Tamang and Shah 2011) and many girls are married by 18 (Puri, Shah and Tamang 2010, Puri, Tamang and Shah 2011, United Nations Populations Fund 2013). Some are married before puberty (Puri, Shah and Tamang 2010, Puri, Tamang and Shah 2011).

Indeed, Nepal appears to have one of the highest rates of child marriage in south Asia (United Nations Children's Fund (UNICEF) 2019). UNICEF data notes that one-third (33%) of 20–24-year-old women in Nepal who were married as at 2019 had done so before the age of 18, and that one-quarter of those (8% of 20–24 year old women) were married before the age of 15 years (UNICEF 2022). The corresponding figure for 20–24-year-old men who were married before the age of 18 is 9%. The incidence of marriage before being 18 years old is higher in rural regions – 39% of married 20–24-year-old women compared with 30% living in urban areas. Data from Nepal's 2011 Census[2] tells a similar story: 23% of 15–19-year-old girls were, or had been, married (which corresponds to about one-third of married 20–24-year-old women[3]). The corresponding figure for boys is 7%. The Census data also shows a clear difference between the urbanized Kathmandu district and the rest of the country (Table 2.3): 10% of 15–19-year-old girls were, or had been, married vs. 24% in the rest of the country. The difference also applies for 15–19-year-old boys: 2% in the Kathmandu district were, or had been, married vs. 8% in the rest of the country. We can infer that the cultural imperative for early marriage remained strong in the last decade, notwithstanding government efforts to change it.

Girls in rural districts often end up married by arrangement to older men, taken to live in his village, and may be beaten or abused if they do not submit to the demands of their husbands or in-laws (Crawford 2017). Wife-beating is considered acceptable in village life and need not be explained or justified (Cameron 1998, Bennett 2002, Crawford 2017). In Brahmin/Chettri, Tamang, Tharu, and Muslim communities of Nepal, the prevalence of intimate partner violence – including sexual

Table 2.3 Number of females and males – 2011 Nepal Census selected data

FEMALE	10–14 yrs			15–19 yrs		
	All	*Kath-mandu*	*Other districts*	*All*	*Kath-mandu*	*Other districts*
Total	1,710,794	78,213	1,632,581	1,488,789	91,340	1,397,449
Married / Married before	19,145	508	18,637	345,469	9,392	336,077
MALE	10–14 yrs			15–19 yrs		
	All	*Kath-mandu*	*Other districts*	*All*	*Kath-mandu*	*Other sistricts*
Total	1,764,630	87,466	1,677,164	1,443,661	110,834	1,332,827
Married / Married before	8,020	268	7,752	102,848	2,660	100,188

coercion and violence – may be up to one in two of uneducated married women in rural regions (Puri, Shah and Tamang 2010, Puri, Tamang and Shah 2011, Puri et al. 2012, Dalal, Wang and Svanstrom 2014). Due to the social value placed on marriage, young women are sometimes lured by men offering marriage but are subsequently sold to brothels in India (Samarasinghe 2008).

It is a constitutional right in Nepal to be able to choose a life partner. However, most marriages in Nepal are arranged by parents (Diamond-Smith et al. 2020) and take place along religious and ethnicity/caste lines (Thapa 1989, Diamond-Smith et al. 2020). Marriage is traditionally arranged by a girl's parents in negotiation with the groom's family and girls are given little say in the process (Hennink and Simkhada (2004), though this is changing – some couples do get to know one another beforehand (Diamond-Smith et al. 2020). Moreover, there is a slow transition away from "arranged" to "love" marriages whereby individuals have more freedom to choose who to marry, but even this is mostly with parental consent (Puri, Shah and Tamang 2010: 1875–6). Parents can also agree to the marriage of their child who is under the age of 18. Traditionally, newly married women live with their husband's family (Sah 2008, Diamond-Smith et al. 2020) and come under the control of their mother-in-law, which is a continuing tradition even in love marriages (Allendorf 2017, Diamond-Smith et al. 2020). A Hindu marriage is not dissolvable and is supposed to subsist beyond death (Mittra and Kumar 2004). In the past, when a man died, the wife was also burned on his funeral pyre in a tradition knows as *sati*, prescribed in the MA of 1854. Due to Hindu religious values, women also have "an attitude of resigned acceptance of the difficulties of life" (Eller and Mahat 2003 p. 58).

Although the dowry system was outlawed in Nepal's Constitution of 2015, the practice of the bride's family giving money and gifts to the groom's family at marriage (Sah 2008) is still common, especially in the Terai region (Niraula and Morgan 1996, Diamond-Smith et al. 2020). An inadequate dowry may be a factor in subsequent domestic violence (Naved and Persson 2010, Pun et al. 2016, Diamond-Smith et al. 2020). The prospect of providing a dowry may lead to parents considering girls to be an economic burden (Deane 2010, Crawford 2017), though once married they are no longer one (Singh 1990).

The dowry brought by the bride is meant to be proportional to the educational level of the groom which, given an expectation to be married, reinforces the priority to educate boys over girls (Paudel 2011). Child marriage also diminishes educational opportunities for girls – they are often also taken out of school to marry (Waszak, Thapa and Davey 2003, Pokharel, Kulczyki and Shakya 2006, Regmi, Simkhada and van Teijlingen 2010) and, even when not, the domestic responsibilities associated with early marriage and motherhood disrupts schooling (Waszak, Thapa and Davey 2003, Hamal Gurung 2014, Crawford 2017).

Women from disadvantaged ethnic groups such as Dalit, Janjati (indigenous), and Muslims, related to the Madhesi, Brahmin/Chettri and other castes, are more likely to get pregnant during adolescence (Gurung et al. 2020) The likelihood of getting pregnant is linked to a lack of access to education (Devkota et al. 2018, Langer et al. 2019). The health consequences of getting pregnant in adolescence are likely to be poor for mother and baby: prolonged labour, premature birth, bearing a small baby for one's gestational age, and having a baby with major congenital malformation (Gurung et al. 2020). Recently, a lack of education has been shown to be a big factor in adolescent pregnancy in a Dalit (untouchable) community in midwest Nepal (Devkota et al. 2018).

Son preference

In Hinduism, women are expected to conceive as soon as possible after marriage to prove their fertility. This means that adolescent marriage is associated with adolescent childbearing (Mittra and Kumar 2004). As part of living in the husband's home and community (Brunson 2016), they are expected to bear sons (Crawford 2017). Indeed, it is important for the wife's first-born child to be a boy (Paudel 2011). If not, she may have to give birth to many children until waiting for a boy to come (Paudel 2011) because at least one son is expected in the family (Rai et al. 2014). Boys are more valued because they are expected to look after their parents as they age, and they are the only ones who can perform funeral rites (Yue, O'Donnell and Sparks 2010, Crawford 2017). Therefore, it is a both practical necessity and a religious duty to have a son (Crawford 2017). However, political and social change following the Maoist Civil War (1996–2006) have brought economic hardship, and parents may find themselves continuing to look after their sons rather than their sons looking after them (Brunson 2016, Ong, Mellor and Chettri 2021).

A possible indication of the cultural value of boys over girls is the disparity in the literacy rates between them, presumably reflecting the disparity in the opportunity for schooling. The disparity is marked for

Table 2.4 Literacy rates of select age groups (Nepal Annual Household Survey 2016/17) (Central Bureau of Statistics 2019)

Age group	Urban		Rural	
	Female	*Male*	*Female*	*Male*
15–19 years	96%	97%	89%	96%
25–29 years	83%	94%	68%	88%
35–39 years	68%	90%	40%	76%
45–49 years	42%	84%	25%	65%
55–59 years	32%	62%	18%	52%
60 years & over	10%	48%	6%	39%

age groups older than 25 years as at 2016–17, and progressively worse with age (see Table 2.4). Literacy rates are lower in rural districts and their gender disparity is more pronounced. Government action to improve literacy in recent years explains the closing of the literacy gap with younger age groups.

The devaluing of girls is so strong in Nepal that it is depicted in a Nepali proverb: "*Choriko janma, hareko karma*" – to be born a daughter is of ill fate/poor destiny (Kondos 2004). Girls may also be made to feel guilty by their social environment for being born female, leading to low self-esteem (Singh 1990, Crawford 2017). In the Terai plains bordering India, some communities see the birth of a daughter as a curse and "the whole neighbourhood weeps when a daughter is born" (Sharma 1986: 63). Some ethnic groups do not view women as human and will respond to the birth of a female child by saying "nothing was born" (Schroeder 2004: 717).

It is not surprising then that the birth of daughter can lead to emotional abuse, and perhaps threats of physical harm, by husbands and mothers-in-law for bearing girls (Ong, Mellor and Chettri 2019) and, if so, women may take to hiding contraceptive taking from husbands – better to avoid the chance of having a daughter even if it means not having a chance of having a boy (Ong 2018). The issues with son-preference have led to high rates of female infanticide, sex selection via ultrasound, and illegal and forced abortion of girls, though the practices are reportedly declining in Nepal (Solotaroff and Pande 2014). Although fertility rates are declining in Nepal, the issues with son-preference are not (Brunson 2010). If couples take time to conceive, the wife is called *tharangi* (infertile), which is considered to be unlucky (Waszak, Thapa and Davey 2003).

Premarital sex and sexual intercourse

In Hinduism, women's sexuality is believed to endanger and affect men's sexuality (Bennett 2002, Crawford 2017) as it is viewed as a source of pollution (Höfer 2004). Women are expected to be modest in relation to matters of sexuality deferring to husbands for sexual knowledge and direction (Poudel and Carryer 2010) and are stigmatized for knowing about sex (Kaufman, Harman and Shrestha 2012). Discussing reproductive health is a sensitive topic for women and girls (Kaufman, Harman and Shrestha 2012, Harman, Kaufman and Shrestha 2014, Menger et al. 2014) and "there are strong social sanctions about communicating across caste lines" (Kaufman, Harman and Shrestha 2012: 328). In fact, communication between a young woman and her husband on sexuality issues is rare (Puri, Shah and Tamang 2010: 1876). Many women believe it is their *dharma* (defined as religion, moral duty, and universal law) to obey, respect, and please their husbands (Cameron 1998, Bennett 2002, Puri, Tamang and Shah 2011). In Nepal, sex has been, and continues to be, largely a male domain (Ahearn 2001). Women are expected to adhere to proprietous values, control their speech, defer their personal gratification, and subordinate their desires (Pigg and Pike 2004, Kaufman and Crawford 2011) especially in relation to their duties to husband and family (Kaufman and Crawford 2011).

Prior to marriage, social, intimate, and sexual relationships between men and women are not viewed as acceptable in Nepali society (Mathur, Malhotra and Mehta 2001, Puri, Shah and Tamang 2010, Regmi, Simkhada and van Teijlingen 2010, Hamal Gurung 2014) nor are multiple marriages and marriage separation (Joshi 2004). Women are expected to be virgins at marriage (Eller and Mahat 2003, Waszak, Thapa and Davey 2003, Samarasinghe 2008, Tamang 2011) and monogamous afterwards (Eller and Mahat 2003). One of the issues sustaining the tradition of early marriage is that the young girl is sexually pure at marriage (Bennett 2002, Samarasinghe 2008, Jafarey, Mainali and Montes 2020). Young girls are also often kept at home until they marry because of this (Waszak, Thapa and Davey 2003).

If it becomes known that a woman has engaged in premarital sex, she is stigmatized (Eller and Mahat 2003, Samarasinghe 2008) as a whore (Regmi, Simkhada and van Teijlingen 2010) including by her husband (Ong, Mellor and Chettri 2021). The term for whore – *wesyā* or *besyā* (women who have who have slept with three men in her life) (Höfer 2004: 41) appears in the MA of 1854. The more men the woman has slept with, the more she is devalued (Höfer 2004). A woman's marriageability is also reduced if she is found to have had premarital sex. She is viewed to be "impure" or, *bigriyo* (ruined) (Pike 2002: 266) and her *ijjat* (family honour and prestige) is lost (Pike 2002: 270).

As with much else of Nepalese culture, these constructions have roots in the Parbatiya (Brahmin/Chhetri) Hindu beliefs and traditions, long enforced by the MA of 1854. The MA of 1854 has much to say about sex. Its "Six Rules of Forbidden Sexual Intercourse" establish sexual privileges and obligations along the lines of caste, gender, and relationship status (Höfer 2004). There are rules about: sodomy; incest; intercourse within pure castes, within impure castes, and between the pure and impure castes; the relationship of a woman of a higher caste status than the man; and rules for women in general (Höfer 2004). There are rules governing sexual relations between a woman and man in the privacy of their home (Doniger 1991), between a woman of a higher caste than the man, and between both partners in the case of adultery (Höfer 2004). Rule 5 largely prohibits women from seeking sex (Höfer 2004). No such constraints apply to men. Even today, men who engage in premarital sex are considered "prestigious" (Regmi, Simkhada and van Teijlingen 2010: 63). Having sex with a commercial sex worker is not considered to affect a single man's virginity nor is the married man viewed to commit adultery with one, because sex with a sex worker is not believed to be "real sex" (Hannum 1997, Eller and Mahat 2003).

To sum up, the attitudes to sex established by MA of 1854 have evolved to shape a culture today where premarital sex and extramarital sex for men is permitted (Eller and Mahat 2003) and indeed these, together with polygamy and divorce, are widely practised by the diverse ethnic groups of Nepal (Joshi 2004). For Nepalese men, in particular, there is, then, a hypocritical disparity between commonly professed Hindu ideals of sexual conduct on the one hand, and the permissiveness spawned under the cover of Hindu patriarchal doctrine on the other.

Stigmatization, oppression, and marginalization of sex-trafficked women in Nepal

In Nepal, sex work as an occupation is viewed as "morally reprehensible" (Pike 2002) because it deviates from the Nepali "ideal" (Samarasinghe 2008) of a girl's virginity at marriage. Women who engage in sex work or who are forced into sex work are severely stigmatized (Hennink and Simkhada 2004). A common phrase in relation to women and girls involved in sex work in Nepal is "*Ke garne chori cheli dimma jastai hunchha, ekchoti futepachhi, futyo, futyo*" (What to do? Unmarried women/girls are like eggs, once broken they never rejoin, you cannot join them) (Hennink and Simkhada 2004). This stigma grounds them as an oppressed caste (Pike 2002, Samarasinghe 2008): *Acchoots*, Dalit, low caste, untouchable. The stigmatization persists despite Nepal's 2006 declaration to be "an 'untouchability free' country" (Vasily 2009: 216). Nepal's current Constitution of 2015 states (at section 24 "Right against untouchability and discrimination"): "No person shall be subjected to any form of untouchability or discrimination in any private and public places on grounds of his or her origin, caste, tribe, community, profession, occupation or physical condition" (Nepal Law Commission 2020: 13).

Three groups of women are profoundly affected by this stigma: Bādi, Deuki, and sex-trafficked women. The Bādi were originally (low caste) musicians forced into sex work by social, economic, and political upheaval in the 1950s, and whose daughters still remain trapped in that environment (Frederick 2000, Pike 2000, Pike 2002, Pigg and Pike 2004). The Deuki women are those subjected to a Hindu religious tradition in which parents "marry" a daughter to a deity or a temple (Shankar 1994, Pike 1999, Pike 2002, Samarasinghe 2008, Verma 2010). This marriage generally takes place before puberty and the girl is then required to provide sexual service to upper caste members of the community, leading "a life of a cheap prostitute with a religious sanction" (Shankar 1994: 17). Women who are trafficked into the sex industry in Nepal or India are stigmatized by mere association with the sex industry even if they have not actually engaged in sexual intercourse. The stigma is worse if they contracted human immunodeficiency virus, acquired immunodeficiency syndrome (HIV/AIDS), and worst if HIV/AIDS was contracted in India (Subedi 2009).

In south Asia generally, once a woman is branded as a prostitute, through derogatory words for whore, the stigma cannot be retracted even in older age and is often passed onto children (Blanchet 1996). The consequences for women and girls who work, or have worked, in the entertainment industry that acts as a front for the sex industry in Nepal is discrimination from landlords who refuse to rent rooms, unkind remarks from shopkeepers, police, and customers, and malicious gossip from villagers (Frederick, Basynet and Aguettant 2010). To note, it is an extreme norm violation to live alone in Nepal (Crawford and Kaufman 2008), a situation often connoted with being a sex worker (Frederick 2012). According to Frederick (2005: 328), "families fear that trafficking returnees will shame the family, spoil their daughters, continue to conduct prostitution in the village, and ruin the family's opportunity to arrange good marriages for their children". As is so clearly stated in the MA of 1854, the consequences of incest, adultery, rape, perversion, and pre-marital sex affect the people immediately involved, their children, and the following generation, and even their own caste members (Höfer 2004). That is, the stigma has a wide and an inter-generational effect.

While there have been attempts to address the stigma of trafficked women (Frederick 2005), changing attitudes is difficult and progress is slow (Frederick, Basynet and Aguettant 2010). Sex trafficking dates back to the Rana Rule (1846–1951) when girls from the hilly districts surrounding the Kathmandu Valley "were 'brought' to the palaces as maid servants [*susaaray*] and as concubines [*bhitrini*] to provide sex for the members of the Rana regime" (Samarasinghe 2008: 71). Many girls were taken to India when the Ranas were overthrown in 1951, after which sex trafficking to India purportedly began. It is believed that a trafficking network had by then been established with the sex industry in Nepal (Samarasinghe 2008, Subedi 2009). By 1951, it was a Nepali "custom" to deliver women and girls into the hands of brokers (usually people known to them) to be trafficked, indicating wide social acceptance of it (Poudel and Carryer 2000). The practice has its own Nepali term "*Cheli Beti Bech Bikhan*" (the buying and selling of girls) (Joshi 2004). As Crawford (2017: 144) notes, sex trafficking "is part of a larger social acceptance of violence against women and girls". That itself has its foundations in Hindu patriarchal norms fostered by the MA of 1854, and the Rana Rule, that created and enforced it; it is regarded by many Nepalese people as one of tyranny, debauchery, economic deprivation, and religious persecution (Brown 1996). In Nepal, "the trafficking of women and girls is believed to be in such a state that some even believe it will never end" (Deane 2010: 509). Even the media fears reporting on it as "a newspaper story would be 'tantamount to a 'suicide mission' for the journalist" (Samarasinghe 2008: 85).

Conclusion

This chapter discusses the form of Hinduism that is practised in Nepal – Parbatiya Hinduism – which was, for over 100 years, embedded in Nepali society through an ancient Hindu legal code, the Muluki Ain of 1854. This produced a heavily patriarchal society, with women being considered lesser than men from birth and expected to depend on men from birth to death. Women are affected by Hinduism and its patriarchal norms across their reproductive lives – becoming untouchable at menstruation and childbirth, being expected to marry as girls, and many accepting the decisions of their parents on whom they are to marry. They are expected to bear children soon after they marry. Sons are preferred, given the place they play in Hindu rituals at death and their expected role in looking after aging parents. While there are strict rules around premarital sex and sex for women, sexual permissiveness is pervasive for men. The stigma attached to premarital sex is magnified for sex-trafficked women on the assumption of sex with multiple men. It extends to the woman's family and village community, hence sometimes leading to being disowned by family and community, especially so if she HIV/AIDS. Perhaps, worse of all, it carries on intergenerationally.

Notes

1 There are various views on the meaning of *chaupadi*. For example, some researchers say *chau* means menstruation and *padi* means women (Robinson 2015). However, others say the roots of the words come from Raute (a Nepali indigenous group) dialect where *chhau* is defined as "untouchable, unclean or impure" and *padi* refers to "being or becoming".
2 At the time of writing, the corresponding data from the 2021 Nepal Census was not yet available.
3 This is comparing the 15–19-year-old cohort (total female population of 1.5 million) with the 20–24-year-old one (1.3 million, 73% married), and so not the same as the UNICEF analysis, but indicates a similar proportionality.

References

Adhikari, P. et al. 2007. Knowledge and practice regarding menstrual hygiene in rural adolescent girls of Nepal. *Kathmandu Medical College Journal,* 5(3),19, 382–6.
Adhikari, R. 2020. Bringing an end to deadly "menstrual huts" is proving difficult in Nepal. *BMJ,* 368.
Ahearn, L. 2001. *Invitations to love: literacy, love letters and social change in Nepal.* Ann Arbor: University of Michigan Press.
Allendorf, K. 2017. Like her own: ideals and experiences of the Mother-In-law/daughter-in-law relationship. *Journal of Family Issues,* 38(15), 2102–27.
Archarya, I., Shakya, M. and Sthapit, S. 2011. Menstrual knowledge and forbidden activities among the Rural Adolescent Girls. *Education and Development* (Special Issue), 107–25. https://www.cerid.org/ [Accessed 20 April 2022].
Batyra, E. and Pesando L.M. 2021. Trends in child marriage and new evidence on the selective impact of changes in age-at-marriage laws on early marriage. *SSM – Population Health,* 14, 100811.
Baumann, S.E., Lhaki, P. and Burke, J.G. 2019. Assessing the role of caste/ethnicity in predicting menstrual knowledge, attitudes, and practices in Nepal. *Global Public Health,* 14(9), 1288–301.
Baumann, S.E. et al., 2021a. Beyond the menstrual shed: exploring caste/ethnic and religious complexities of menstrual practices in Far-West Nepal. *Women's Reproductive Health,* 8(1), 1–28.

Baumann, S.E. et al. 2021b. Is criminalization the answer? Perspectives of community members and police on menstrual seclusion policy in Far-West Nepal. *Health Policy and Planning*, 36(7), 1003–12.

Bennett, L. 1976, *The wives of the rishis: an analysis of the Tij Rishi Panchami Woman' Festival.* Cambridge: University of Cambridge. http://himalaya.socanth.cam.ac.uk/collections/journals/kailash/pdf/kailash_04_02_04.pdf [Accessed 3 April 2021].

Bennett, L. 2002. *Dangerous wives and sacred sisters: social and symbolic roles of high-caste women in Nepal.* 2nd ed. Kathmandu: Mandala Publications.

Bhartiya, A. 2013.Menstruation, religion and society. *International Journal of Social Science and Humanity*, 3(6), 523–7. http://www.ijssh.org/papers/296-B00016.pdf [Accessed 3 April 2021].

Bist, B.S. 2014. The effect of religious hazards in health among menstrual women: a case of far-west Nepal. *The Korean Journal of Public Health*, 51(2), 105–16.

Blanchet, T. 1996, *Lost innocence, stolen childhoods.* Dhaka: University Press Limited, Dhaka.

Brown T. 1996. *The challenge to democracy in Nepal: a political history.* London: Routledge.

Brunson, J. 2010. Son preference in the context of fertility decline: limits to new constructions of gender and kinship in Nepal. *Studies in Family Planning*, 41(2), 89–98. https://www.ncbi.nlm.nih.gov/pmc/articles/PMC4203699/ [Accessed 3 April 2021].

Brunson, J. 2016. *Planning families in Nepal: global and local projects of reproduction.* New Brunswick: Rutgers University Press.

Cameron, M. 1998. *On the edge of the auspicious: gender and caste in Nepal.* Kathmandu: Mandala Publications.

Cardoso, L.F. et al. 2019. Menstrual restriction prevalence and association with intimate partner violence among Nepali women. *BMJ Sexual and Reproductive Health*, 45(1), 38–43.

Central Bureau of Statistics. 2019. *Annual Household Survey 2016/17.* Kathmandu: Government of Nepal. https://nepalindata.com/media/resources/items/20/bAnnual-Household-Survey-2016_17.pdf [Accessed 2 June 2022].

Crawford, M. 2017. International sex trafficking. *Women and Therapy*, 40 (1–2), 101–22.

Crawford, M. and Kaufman, M. 2008. Sex trafficking in Nepal: survivor characteristics and long-term outcomes. *Violence Against Women*, 14 (8), 905–16.

Crawford, M., Menger, L. and Kaufman, M. 2014. "This is a natural process": managing menstrual stigma in Nepal. *Culture, Health and Sexuality*, 16(4), 426–39.

Dahal, K. 2008. Nepalese woman dies after banishment to shed during menstruation. *British Medical Journal*, 337.

Dalal, K., Wang, S. and Svanstrom, L. 2014. Intimate partner violence against women in Nepal: analysis through individual, empowerment, family and societal level factors. *Journal of Research in Health Sciences*, 14(4), 251–7.

De Schutter, O. 2021. *Statement by Professor Olivier De Schutter, United Nations Special Rapporteur on extreme poverty and human rights, on his visit to Nepal.* Geneva: United Nations Human Rights Office of the High Commissioner. https://www.ohchr.org/en/statements/2021/12/statement-professor-olivier-de-schutter-united-nations-special-rapporteur [Accessed 2 June 2022].

Deane, T. 2010. Cross-border trafficking in Nepal and India – violating women's rights. *Human Rights Review*, 11, 491–513.

Devkota, H.R. et al. 2018. Does women's caste make a significant contribution to adolescent pregnancy in Nepal? A study of Dalit and non-Dalit adolescents and young adults in Rupandehi district. *BMC Womens Health*, 8(1), 23.

Diamond-Smith, N.G. et al., 2020. Semi-arranged marriages and dowry ambivalence: Tensions in the changing landscape of marriage formation in South Asia. *Culture, Health and Sexuality*, 22(9), 971–86.

Doniger, W. 1991. Why should a priest tell you whom to marry? A deconstruction of the Laws of Manu. *Bulletin of the American Academy of Arts and Sciences*, 44(1), 18–31.

Eller, L. and Mahat, G. 2003. Psychological factors in Nepali former commercial sex workers with HIV. *Journal of Nursing Scholarship*, 35(1), 53–60.

Frederick, J. 2000. In the family business: Nepal and India. In: J. Frederick, ed., Fallen *angels: the sex workers of South Asia*. New Delhi: Roli Books, 57–63.

Frederick, J. 2005. The status of care, support, social reintegration of trafficked persons in Nepal, as of December 2005. *Tulane Journal of International Compliance and Law*, 14, 316–30. Available from: http://heinonline.org/HOL/LandingPage?handle=hein.journals/tulicl14&div=18&id=&page= [Accessed 3 April 2022].

Frederick, J. 2012. The myth of Nepal-to-India sex trafficking: its creation, its maintenance, and its influence on anti-trafficking interventions. In: K. Kempadoo, J. Sanghera and B. Pattanaik, eds., *Trafficking and prostitution reconsidered: perspectives on migration, sex work and human rights*. 2nd ed. Boulder: Paradigm, 127–47

Frederick, J., Basynet, M. and Aguettant, L. 2010. *Trafficking and exploitation in the entertainment and sex industries in Nepal: a handbook for decision-makers*. Kathmandu: Terres des hommes Foundation. https://www.tdh.ch/sites/default/files/study_trafficking_tdhl_2010.pdf [Accessed 3 April 2021].

Geiser, A. 2005. *Social exclusion and conflict transformation in Nepal: women, Dalit and ethnic Groups: FAST Country Risk Profile Nepal*. Bern: Swiss Peace. https://raonline.ch/pages/np/pdf/npsoc_women01.pdf [Accessed 2 June 2022].

Grossman-Thompson, B. 2016. Protection and paternalism: narratives of Nepali women migrants and the gender politics of discriminatory labour migration policy. *Refuge: Canada's Journal on Refugees,* 32(3), 40–8.

Grossman-Thompson, B. 2017. "My honor will be erased": working-class women, purchasing power, and the perils of modernity in urban Nepal. *Journal of Women in Culture and Society,* 42(2), 485–507.

Gurung, R. et al. 2020. The burden of adolescent motherhood and health consequences in Nepal. *BMC pregnancy and childbirth*, 20(1), 1–7.

Hamal Gurung, S. 2014. Sex trafficking and the sex trade industry: the processes and experiences of Nepali Women. *Journal of Intercultural Studies*, 35(2), 163–81.

Hannum, J. 1997. *AIDS in Nepal: communities confronting an emerging epidemic in Nepal.* New York: Seven Stories Press.

Harman, J., Kaufman, M. and Shrestha, D. 2014. Evaluation of the "Let's Talk" safer sex intervention in Nepal. *Journal of Health Communication*, 19(8), 1–11.

Hennink, M. and Simkhada, P. 2004. Sex trafficking in Nepal: context and process. *Asian and Pacific Migration*, 13(3), 305–38.

Höfer, A. 2004. *The caste hierarchy and the state in Nepal: a study of the Muluki Ain of 1854.* Kathmandu: Himal Books.

International Fund for Agricultural Development (IFAD). 2022. *Nepal.* Rome: IFAD. https://www.ifad.org/en/web/operations/w/country/nepal [Accessed 2 June 2022].

Jafarey, S., Mainali, R. and Montes, R.G. 2020. Age at marriage, social norms, and female education in Nepal. *Review of Development Economics*, 24(3), 878–909.

Joshi, S. 2004. "Cheli-beti" discourses of trafficking and constructions of gender, citizenship and nation in modern Nepal. In: S. Srivatsava, ed., *Sexual sites and seminal attitudes: sexualities, masculinities and culture in South Asia.* New Delhi: Sage, 242–70.

Kaphle, S. 2021. *Socio-cultural insights of childbirth in South Asia: stories of women in the Himalayas.* Milton: Routledge.

Kaufman, M. and Crawford, M. 2011. Research and activism review: sex trafficking in Nepal: a review of intervention and prevention programs. *Violence Against Women*, 17(5) 651–5.

Kaufman, M., Harman, J. and Shrestha, D. 2012. "Let's talk about sex": development of a sexual health program for Nepali women. *AIDS Education and Prevention*, 24(4), 327–38.

Kondos, V. 2004. *On the ethos of Hindu women: issues, taboos and forms of expression.* Kathmandu: Mandala Publications.

Lamichhane, P. et al. 2011. Women's status and violence against young married women in rural Nepal. *BMC Women's Health*, 1(11) 1–9.

Langer J.A. et al. 2019. Gender and child behavior problems in rural Nepal: differential expectations and responses. *Scientific Reports*, 9(1), 7662. https://www.nature.com/articles/s41598-019-43972-3 [Accessed 3 April 2021].

Mahon, T. and Fernandes, M. 2010. Menstrual hygiene in South Asia: a neglected issue for WASH (water, sanitation and hygiene) programmes. *Gender and Development*, 18(1), 99–113.

Mathur, S., Malhotra, A. and Mehta M. 2001. Adolescent girls' aspirations and reproductive health in Nepal. *Reproductive Health Matters*, 9(17), 63–84.

Menger, L. et al. 2014. Unveiling the silence: women's sexual health and experiences in Nepal. *Culture, Health and Sexuality*, 17(3), 359–73.

Milner, M. 1994. *Status and sacredness: a general theory of status relations and an analysis of Indian culture*. Oxford: Oxford University Press on Demand.

Ministry of Foreign Affairs. 2022. *Geography of Nepal*. Tokyo: Government of Nepal. https://jp.nepalembassy.gov.np/geography-of-nepal/ [Accessed 2 June 2022].

Mittra, S. and Kumar, B., eds. *Encyclopaedia of Women in South Asia: India, Volume 1*. Delhi: Kalpaz Publications.

Mukherjee, A. et al. 2020. Perception and practices of menstruation restrictions among urban adolescent girls and women in Nepal: a cross-sectional survey. *Reproductive Health*,17(1), 1–10.

Narayan, A. and Purkayastha, B. 2009. *Living our religions: Hindu and Muslim South Asian American women narrate their experiences*. Boulder, CO: Kumarian Press.

Naved, R.T. and Persson, L.A. 2010. Dowry and spousal physical violence against women in Bangladesh. *Journal of Family issues*, 31(6), 830–56.

Nepal Law Commission. 2011. *The Caste-Based Discrimination and Untouchability (Offence and Punishment) Act, 2068 (2011)*. Kathmandu: Government of Nepal. https://adsdatabase.ohchr.org/IssueLibrary/NEPA L_Caste%20Based%20Discrimination%20and%20Untouchability%20(Offe nce%20and%20Punishment)%20Act.pdf [Accessed 2 June 2022].

Nepal Law Commission. 2020. *The Constitution of Nepal*. Kathmandu: Government of Nepal. https://www.lawcommission.gov.np/en/wp-content/ uploads/2021/01/Constitution-of-Nepal.pdf [Accessed 2 June 2022].

Niraula, B.B. and Morgan, S.P. 1996. Marriage formation, post-marital contact with natal kin and autonomy of women: evidence from two Nepali settings. *Population Studies*, 50(1), 35–50.

Ong T., Mellor, D. and Chettri, S. 2019. Multiplicity of stigma: the experiences, fears and knowledge of young trafficked women in Nepal. *Sexual and Reproductive health Matters*, 27(3), 32–48.

Ong, T., Mellor, D. and Chettri, S. 2021. "Females are always dominated and disregarded by males, just because they are female": the continuation of patriarchal norms for young trafficked women in Nepal. *Culture, Health and Sexuality*, 1–16.

Ong, P. 2018. *Reproductive health for the marginalised: knowledge of young women trafficked into the sex industry in Nepal*. Thesis (PhD). Deakin University.

Paudel, S. 2011. Women's concerns within Nepal's patriarchal justice system. *Ethics in Action*, 5(6), 30–6. http://www.humanrights.asia/wp-content/uplo ads/2019/03/Nepal%E2%80%99s-patriarchal-justice-system.pdf [Accessed 29 April 2022].

Pike, L. 1999. Innocence danger and desire: representations of sex workers in Nepal. *Global Reproductive Health Forum*, 2, 1–16.

Pike, L. 2000. Home economics: Nepal. In: J. Frederick, ed., *Fallen angels: the sex workers of South Asia*. New Delhi: Roli Books, 81–4.

Pike, L. 2002. Sex work and socialisation in a moral world: conflict and change in Bādī Communities in Western Nepal. In: L. Manderson and P. Liamputtong, eds, *Coming of age in South and South East Asia: youth, courtship and sexuality*. Richmond: Curzon Press, Richmond, 228–48.

Pigg, S. and Pike, L. 2004. Knowledge, attitudes, beliefs and practices. In: S. Srivatsava, ed, *Sexual sites and seminal attitudes: sexualities, masculinities and culture in South Asia*. New Delhi: Sage.

Pokharel, S., Kulczyki, A. and Shakya, S. 2006. School-based sex education in Western Nepal: uncomfortable for both teachers and students. *Reproductive Health Matters*, 14(28), 156–61.

Posner, J. et al. 2009. Development of leadership self-efficacy and collective efficacy: adolescent girls across castes as peer educators in Nepal. *Global Public Health*, 4(3) 284–302.

Poudel, P. and Carryer, J. 2000. Girl trafficking, HIV/AIDS, and the position of women in Nepal. *Gender and Development*, 8(2), 74–9.

Pradhan, R. 2005. *The Ain of 1854 and after legal pluralism, models of society and ethnicity in Nepal*. Berlin: ResearchGate. https://www.researchgate.net/publication/283902011_The_Ain_of_1854_and_after_Legal_pluralism_models_of_society_and_ethnicity_in_Nepal [Accessed 2 June 2022].

Pradhan, R. 2011. Ethnicity, caste and a pluralist society. In: K. Visweswaran, ed., *Perspectives on modern South Asia: a reader in culture, history, and representation*. Malden: Wiley-Blackwell, 100–11.

Pun, K.D. et al. 2016. Community perceptions on domestic violence against pregnant women in Nepal: a qualitative study. *Global Health Action*, 9(1), 31964.

Puri, M., Shah, I. and Tamang, J. 2010. Exploring the nature and reasons for sexual violence within marriage among young women in Nepal. *Journal of Interpersonal Violence*, 25(10), 1873–92.

Puri, M., Tamang, J. and Shah, I. 2011. Suffering in silence: consequences of sexual violence within marriage among young women in Nepal. *BMC Public Health*, 11(1), 1–10. doi: 10.1186/1471-2458-11-29.

Puri, M. et al. 2012. The prevalence and determinants of sexual violence against young married women by husbands in rural Nepal. *BMC Research Notes*, 5(1), 1–13.

Rai, P. et al. 2014. Effect of gender preference on fertility: cross-sectional study among women of Tharu community from rural area of eastern region of Nepal. *Reproductive Health*, 11(1), 1–6.

Ranabhat, C. et al. 2015. Chhaupadi culture and reproductive health of women in Nepal. *Asia Pacific Journal of Public Health*, 27(7), 785–95.

Regmi, P., Simkhada, P. and van Teijlingen, E. 2010. "Boys remain prestigious, girls become prostitutes": Socio-cultural context of relationships and sex among young people in Nepal. *Global Journal of Health Science*, 2(1), 60–72.

Robinson, H. 2015. Chaupadi: the affliction of menses in Nepal. *International Journal of Women's Dermatology*, 1(4), 193–4. https://www.ncbi.nlm.nih.gov/pmc/articles/PMC5419759/ [Accessed 3 April 2021].

Sah, N. 2008. How useful are the demographic surveys in explaining the determinants of early marriage of girls in the Terai of Nepal?. *Journal of Population Research*, 25(2), 207–22.

Samarasinghe, V. 2008. *Female sex trafficking in Asia: the resilience of patriarchy in a changing world.* New York: Routledge.

Sapkota, D. et al. 2013. Knowledge and practices regarding menstruation among school going adolescents of rural Nepal. *Journal of Kathmandu Medical College*, 2(3) iss. 5, 122–8. https://jkmc.com.np/ojs3/index.php/jour nal/article/view/822/810 [Accessed 3 April 2022].

Schroeder, E. 2004. Nepal. In: R. Francoeur and R. Noonan, eds, *The Continuum Complete International Encyclopedia of Sexuality*. Bloomington: The Kinsey Institute, 714–24. https://kinseyinstitute.org/pdf/ccies-nepal.pdf [Accessed 3 April 2022].

Shahi, P. et al. 2019. Child marriage: knowledge, practice and its attributed consequences among early married women in Jumla, Nepal. *Asian Pacific Journal of Health Science*, 6(1), 140–8.

Shankar, J. 1994. *Devadasi cult: a sociological analysis*. New Delhi: Ashish Publishing House.

Sharma, K. 1986. Bondages of Nepalese women. *Community Development Journal*, 21(1), 62–5.

Sharma, S. et al. 2016. Dirty and 40 days in the wilderness: eliciting childbirth and postnatal cultural practices and beliefs in Nepal. *BMC Pregnancy and Childbirth*, 16(1), 1–12.

Sharma, B. and Schultz, K. 2019. Woman Killed by Fire in Menstruation Hut, as Nepal Fights a Tradition. *New York Times*, 2 February. https://www.nyti mes.com/2019/02/02/world/asia/nepal-menstruation-hut-death-chhaupadi. html [Accessed 3 April 2021].

Singh, I. 1990. Sociocultural factors affecting girl children in Nepal. *Asia Pacific Journal of Public Health*, 4(4), 251–4.

Solotaroff, J. and Pande, R. 2014. *Violence against women and girls: lessons from South Asia.* Washington: World Bank Group. https://openknowledge.world bank.org/handle/10986/20153 [Accessed 3 April 2021].

Standing, K. and Parker, S. 2017. Girl's and women's rights to menstrual health in Nepal. In: N. Mahtab, I. Barsha, M. Islam and I. Binte Wahid, eds, *Handbook of research on women's issues and rights in the developing world.* Hershey: IGI Global, 156–68.

Subedi, G. 2009. Trafficking in girls and women in Nepal for commercial sexual exploitation: emerging gaps and concerns. *Pakistan Journal of Women's Studies: Alam-e-Niswan*, 16(1/2), 121–46.

Tamang, S. 2011. The politics of "developing Nepali women". In: K. Visweswaran, ed., *Perspectives on Modern South Asia: a reader in culture, history, and representation.* Malden: Wiley-Blackwell.

Thapa, S. 1989. The Ethnic Factor in the Timing of Family Formation in Nepal. *Asia-Pacific Population Journal*, 4(1), 3–34.

United Nations Nepal (UN Nepal). 2020. *Harmful Practices in Nepal: Report on Community Perceptions.* Kathmandu: UN Nepal. https://un.org.np/resou rce/harmful-practices-nepal-report-community-perceptions [Accessed 2 June 2021].

United Nations Children's Fund (UNICEF). 2022. *UNICEF Data Warehouse.* New York: UNICEF. https://data.unicef.org/resources/data_explorer/unice f_f/?ag=UNICEF&df=PT&ver=1.0&dq=NPL.PT_F_15-19_MRD+PT_F _20-24_MRD_U15+PT_F_20-24_MRD_U18+PT_M_15-19_MRD+PT_ M_20-24_MRD_U18......&startPeriod=2016&endPeriod=2022 [Accessed 2 June 2022].

United Nations Children's Fund. 2019. *Nepal profile – UNFPA–UNICEF Global Programme to End Child Marriage.* Kathmandu: UNICEF. https:// www.unicef.org/media/88831/file/Child-marriage-Nepal-profile-2019.pdf [Accessed 28 April 2022].

United Nations Conference on Trade and Development. 2022. *General profile: Nepal.* [online], Geneva: UNICEF. https://unctadstat.unctad.org/Cou ntryProfile/GeneralProfile/en-GB/524/GeneralProfile524.pdf [Accessed 2 June 2022].

United Nations Population Fund. 2013. *UNFPA strategy on adolescents and youth: towards realising the full potential of adolescents and youth.* New York: United Nations Population Fund. http://www.unfpa.org/sites/default/files/ resource-pdf/UNFPA%20Adolescents%20and%20Youth%20Strategy.pdf [Accessed 29 April 2022].

United Nations Populations Fund, United Nations Children's Fund and United Nations Volunteers (UNFPA, UNICEF, UNRCO). 2020. *Literature Review of Harmful Practices in Nepal.* Pulchowk: UNFPA Nepal. https:// nepal.unfpa.org/en/publications/literature-review-harmful-practices-nepal [Accessed 2 June 2022].

Vasily, L. 2009. Struggles against domination: forms of Nepali Dalit activism. In: D. Gellner, ed., *Ethnic Activism and Civil Society in South Asia.* New Delhi: Thousand Oaks, 215–40.

Verma, A. 2010. Trafficking in India. In. K. McCabe and A. Manian, eds, *Sex Trafficking: A Global Perspective.* Lanham, MD: Lexington Books, 181–98.

Waszak, C., Thapa, S. and Davey, J. 2003. Influence of gender norms on the reproductive health of adolescents in Nepal – perspectives of youth. In: S. Bott, S. Jejeebhoy, I. Shah and C. Puri, eds, *Towards adulthood: exploring the sexual and reproductive health of adolescents in South Asia.* Geneva: World Health Organisation, 81–5. http://www.who.int/reproductivehealth/publicati ons/adolescence/9241562501/en/ [Accessed 3 April 2021].

World Bank. 2022. *Population total – Nepal.* Washington: World Bank. https:// data.worldbank.org/indicator/SP.POP.TOTL?locations=NP [Accessed 3 May 2022].

Yadav, R.N. et al. 2017. Knowledge, attitude, and practice on menstrual hygiene management among school adolescents. *Journal of Nepal Health Research Council,* 15(3), 212–6.

Yilmaz, S. K., Bohara, A. K. and Thapa, S. 2021. The stressor in adolescence of menstruation: coping strategies, emotional stress and impacts on school absences among young women in Nepal. *International Journal of Environmental Research and Public Health*, 18(17), 8894.

Yue, K., O'Donnell, C. and Sparks, P. 2010. The effect of spousal communication on contraceptive use in Central Terai, Nepal. *Patient Education and Counselling*, 81(3), 402–8.

3 A feminist approach to sensitive research

The inspiration of critical ethnography and participatory action research

Introduction

The quality of life of Nepalese women, and particularly sex-trafficked women, is a long-held concern of mine. It was a lens through which I absorbed the culture in each of my many trips to Nepal. In 2015–16, I had the opportunity to undertake in-depth research into the reproductive health knowledge of young Nepalese sex-trafficked women (Ong 2018, Ong, Mellor and Chettri, 2019, 2020, 2021). The outcome of the research depended heavily on eliciting knowledge, perceptions, and beliefs about reproductive health issues from the women, and therein lay enormous challenges for Western-orientated research methods. For all the support we had in Australia (academic, financial) and Nepal (local partner organizations, local professional expertise), our overriding uncertainty was how we ought to engage with the women to elicit their knowledge and experiences. For Nepalese women, personal sexual and reproductive health issues are extraordinarily sensitive topics and are not freely or casually discussed, let alone with a foreigner – as I would be to them. Compounding this cultural reservedness is, for the women who are the focus of our research, their stigmatization, oppression, and marginalization due to being considered "impure", having been trafficked for sex. I explore the patriarchal and Hindu roots of this in the previous chapter, and note here that it explains, in part, why sexual and reproductive health issues are under-researched in Nepal and that ethical considerations for research loom large.

This chapter describes the research methodology we developed and applied – the Clay Embodiment Research Method (CERM). We look at accommodating cultural sensitivity through inspiration from critical ethnography and participatory action research (PAR) and underlying feminist research methods and feminist theory. After much inquiry and study and drawing on my professional experience and those of others, I realized

DOI: 10.4324/b23275-3

that approaches based on feminist theory were more likely than any other approaches considered to enable us to begin from the experiences of the women and encourage free-flowing discussion and non-verbal communication for this vulnerable group of women in Nepal. Moreover, they provide an effective framework for analysing the data these generate, and for drawing insights from it. These approaches underpin the CERM.

A lens of critical ethnography

I was first drawn to ethnography as an approach for our research. Ethnography is "the branch of anthropology that deals with the systematic description of human cultures" (Pelto 2013: 18). It is a qualitative research method in which researchers study socio/cultural groups to gain a deeper understanding of them (De Laine 1997, Kramer and Adams 2017). It is both a process and a product (Kramer and Adams 2017). The process of "doing ethnography" requires an ethnographer to actively participate in the group to gain an insider's perspective and to share common experiences (Kramer and Adams 2017). The product of "writing ethnography" requires the ethnographer to create an account of the group based on involvement with the group, interviews with group members, and an analysis of group documents such field notes and artefacts (De Laine 1997, Van Maanen 2011, Kramer and Adams 2017).

The concept of ethnography was developed in the mid-1700s, and now includes feminist approaches that focus on women's lives and perspectives. They consider highly gendered settings using methods and writing styles that apply feminist theories and ethics and undertaking analysis through a feminist theoretical lens (Hesse-Biber 2014). Ethnography is well known as a research methodology in Nepal and used by feminist anthropologists and sociologists, such as Mary Cameron (1998) and Lynn Bennett (2002), with illiterate women in rural communities there. However, in Nepal, Seppälä (2020: 83) has recently highlighted "blatant Eurocentrism and deep power imbalances and complexities of ethnographic research". Conventional ethnography describes social conditions as is. For the research with sex-trafficked Nepalese women, I favoured a more contemporary conception of ethnography that acknowledges an historical viewpoint: "Ethnography ... consists of processes and products of research that document what people know, feel and do in a way that situates the phenomena at specific timepoints in the history of individuals lives, including global events and processes" (Handwerker 2001: 7). This incorporates elements of critical ethnography. Critical ethnography explicitly sets out to critique imbalances in power relations, including dominance by, or oppression of, one state or social group over another (Thomas 1993, Palmer and Caldas 2016, Norlander 2017). It is underpinned by critical theory – the use of a social philosophy that focuses on reflective assessment and critique of society and culture to reveal and challenge power structures – as methodological choices and practices of the researcher (Norlander 2017). Whereas both conventional ethnography and critical ethnography refer to a tradition of cultural description and analysis that show meaning by interpretation, critical ethnography includes a reflective process of choosing between making value-laden judgments of meaning and methods to challenge research, policy, and other human actions (Thomas and O'Maolchatha 1989, Thomas 1993). Conventional ethnography describes *what is*; critical ethnography goes a step further and asks *what could be* (Thomas 1993).

Although I was attracted to a critical ethnographic approach, there was a significant drawback in its use in the circumstances of my research in Nepal. All ethnographies generally require researchers to spend long periods in the field to immerse themselves in the social environment of the research. Given the extent of what I aimed to cover, it would ideally require more time than my funding provided. This is not an uncommon situation for ethnographers, leading them to develop innovative methods "to provide routes into understanding other people's lives, experiences, values, social worlds and more that go beyond the classic observational approach" (Pink 2009: 4–5). Critical ethnographers work closely with community members, engage in participatory research, and are involved in ongoing dialogue with those being researched (Palmer and Caldas 2016). It appeared to me that there were "routes into understanding" that need not require the time in the field envisioned by conventional ethnography. This led me to the use of a component of ethnography – participant observation – and applying a critical theoretical lens to its application.

Participant observation can involve taking an active or passive role depending on the research context (Jorgensen 1989, De Laine 1997, DeWalt and DeWalt 2011). It is "highly desirable for the participant observer to perform multiple roles during the course of the project, and gain at least a comfortable degree of rapport, even intimacy, with the people, situations and settings of research" (Jorgensen 1989: 21). Due to the collective culture in Nepal, I envisaged this approach being used actively to firstly, "gain entrée" to the field – to select and describe the human setting of the research and to formulate a strategy for gaining access to it (Jorgenson 1989: 40). Secondly, it would develop rapport and trust with our research participants to enable us to learn about their embodied (body) experiences (personal dimension) and group dynamics (social dimension) in their living environments, and to gain deep insight into the role of culturally embedded patriarchy in their lives. In collective cultures, individuals view themselves as parts of a larger whole, such as family, and are motivated mainly by norms and obligations imposed by the collective entity (Triandis 2018). With my prior knowledge of Nepal, I knew I would be *expected* to immerse myself in the daily lives of the women and girls and that this process would likely take the form of many discussions over cups of *masala chia* (spiced tea), cooking, singing, and dancing, taking part cultural rituals and developing my rudimentary Nepali language skills – and it would be *ramaailo* (fun).

So, the "human setting" of our research called for more than participant observation, however active it may be. We also needed a model of being immersed in the personal and social lives of our research participants yet be apart from it as researchers. We looked to PAR.

The inspiration of participatory action research

Participatory action research, feminist theory and feminist research methods for engaging stigmatized, oppressed, and marginalized women

PAR is an approach to research rather than a research method (Kindon, Pain and Kesby 2007, Pain et al. 2011). The process involves an iterative cycle of research that emphasizes participation, action, research, and social change for justice (Schubotz 2019). It offers potential to work collaboratively with local people to find solutions to their pragmatic problems (Cornwall and Jewkes 1995, Leavy 2017). It aims to empower people affected by the research in the research process. The intention is to make the participant an equal partner with the researcher (Patton 2008, Boyle 2012), and both can gain new knowledge. PAR is reflexive, flexible, and iterative as compared to the rigid linear designs of most conventional science (Cornwall and Jewkes 1995). This means PAR tools and methods can be adapted.

PAR is anchored in feminist theoretical foundations – in feminist research methods, feminist theory, and critical (consciousness) theory (Cornwall and Jewkes 1995). In the study of gender, feminist research recognizes the simultaneous nature of our complex selves and the ways in which multiple aspects of privilege or oppression are exercised at once (Leavy and Harris 2018). Feminist research also recognizes that women's perspectives are important and distinct from men's (Hartsock 1983). While gender is central to defining what feminist research does, it also explores and challenges the power imbalance between the researcher and the researched, is politically driven, has a sense of purpose, aims to remove social inequalities, and enables the experiences of women to guide the entire research process (Hussain and Asad 2012).

One feminist theory that I felt was particularly pertinent to our research is standpoint theory, which posits that knowledge is socially situated. It espouses the idea that research should begin with women's perspectives to generate less partial and distorted accounts of their lives, those of men, and the whole social order (Harding 1993). An underlying belief is that marginalized groups are better positioned to be aware of actual social conditions than the non-marginalized (Harding 2004). Therefore, research that focuses on power relations should begin with the perspectives of the marginalized and/or oppressed to create more objective accounts of the world (Harding 2004). For our research, this was to begin with the perspectives of one of the most stigmatized, oppressed, and marginalized groups of women in Nepal: sex-trafficked women (see Chapter 2). By starting at the bottom of the social hierarchy, complex human relations can become more visible (Hesse-Biber, Leavy and Yaiser 2004).

The basis of PAR then had much that appealed to me for our research. Yet, like ethnography, it requires considerable time in the field. However, the flexibility of PAR meant we could adapt some of its tools and methods to suit our research objectives and circumstances.

Participatory action research and visual arts-based methods: body-mapping and clay as a new medium

PAR encourages the use of visual tools and arts-based methods. Having a creative arts therapist background, I saw how visual and arts-based methods could be used in my research with sex-trafficked Nepalese women. The variety of tools, techniques, and strategies available is virtually limitless and has included community mapping, focus group discussions, gender role analysis, use of drawings, posters, role-play, photography, theatre, and songs. These make research accessible for literate and illiterate populations.

Arts-based methods have recently been noted as important "for contesting hierarchies in research, increasing multivocality, and developing new and more transparent forms of participatory research" (Seppälä, Sarantou and Miettinen 2021: 2). They can be important for decolonizing research practice, yet also produce recolonizing if researchers are not attentive to hierarchies, power imbalances, and ethical concerns (Seppälä, Sarantou and Miettinen 2021) or are otherwise not skilled in their application and use. The use of arts-based methods requires building trust and may require long-term partnership and engagement (Seppälä, Sarantou and Miettinen 2021), something I already had with the Nepalese organizations we would work with in our research (namely Smriti Khadka and Asha Nepal). Moreover, arts-based methods generally require a deep understanding of the specific context and usually only a small number of people can participate (Seppälä, Sarantou and Miettinen 2021). For this reason, they actually suited our research (see Chapter 5).

The arts-based method that I was excited about was body-mapping – a "visual arts-based process" (Jager et al. 2016: 2) – already used for over 30 years in sexual and reproductive health research and training, with women, men, adolescents and youth, and children in individual and group contexts in Australia, Bangladesh, Belgium, Canada, India, Jamaica, Kenya, Nepal, South Africa, USA, Zambia, and Zimbabwe (see Jager et al. 2016, Ong 2018, Ong, Mellor and Chettri 2020 for more information).

There are many variations of body-mapping techniques and applications,[1] and an illustrative example (of both processes, use, and limitations) that is extremely relevant to Nepal is that pioneered by Carol MacCormack (1985), a social anthropologist from the United Kingdom. MacCormack's technique involves providing an outline of a human body on paper to research participants, asking them to draw their reproductive systems within the outline, as a step to exploring their views on various reproductive health issues. It was first used in individual interviews with Jamaican women to elicit their views on contraception, to find out how this affected their utilization of Jamaican family planning services (MacCormack 1985). Her technique has since been adapted by others for different purposes, in different contexts, and with different population groups (see Jager et al. 2016, Ong 2018, Ong, Mellor and Chettri 2020). Although it has not been studied, it seems especially useful in a group environment because it stimulates dynamic discussion (Zaman, Mustaque and Chowdhury1998), though participants may copy each other's work, share misinformation, and the dominance of individuals can detract from its potential (Sturley 2000).

Body-mapping is claimed to be fast (Gazi and Chowdhury 2003) as a data collection method. However, to date, no one appears to have compared its speed and efficiency to that of other qualitative research methods. Indeed, until recently the use of body-mapping has remained largely uncritiqued (see Jager et al. 2016, Ong 2018, Ong, Mellor and Chettri 2020). The assessments that have emerged and my own observations point to at least three risk factors – related to the facilitators – that should be honestly considered before endeavouring to apply body-mapping for the purposes for which it is designed. Briefly, these are: first, the depth of their understanding of the cultural context of the lives of the intended participants; second, their expertise in choice and application of a body-mapping technique; and, third, their preparedness for the elicitation of distress or even trauma of participants during the body-mapping or as a consequence of it. I think the risk of trauma depends on how much distress or trauma is held in the memories that the body-mapping evokes, and on how the memories are evoked. For example, using another body-mapping technique designed by Jane Solomon, an artist from South Africa, participants trace around their body onto cloth (Solomon 2007). This direct engagement with one's body and can elicit trauma, and so is not suitable for use with some population groups (see Jager et al. 2016, Ong 2018, Ong, Mellor and Chettri 2020). It is the reason why Solomon withdrew her once freely available facilitator guide from the internet (Solomon 2020). Notably, this method had never been used in sexual and reproductive health research in Nepal, and I believed it would elicit trauma in our vulnerable research participants.

To date, there have been no reports of trauma elicitation with MacCormack's technique. However, there appears to be no interrogation of the method either. Nevertheless, training in body-mapping facilitation is considered necessary because of issues that can emerge for research participants and facilitators (Jager et al. 2016, Orchard 2017, Ong, Mellor and Chettri 2020, Boydell et al. 2020, Solomon 2020), as is a safe environment for its practice (Stevens and Le Roux 2011, Jager et al. 2016, Orchard 2017, Solomon 2020), because body-mapping is "dangerous emotional terrain" (Solomon 2020: xvii). My observation is that its use by possibly untrained facilitators has been unsuccessful (producing results of little value) and a bare application of its Western perspective may be regarded as (re)colonizing.

Body-mapping with semi-literate and illiterate groups

MacCormack's body-mapping technique was initially attractive for use in my proposed research because it has worked well in some capacities with semi-literate and illiterate populations. Its usefulness here is that it does not rely on verbal descriptions of the body (Kesby and Gwanzura-Ottemöller 2007) – "visual literacy is independent of alphabetic literacy" (Zaman, Mustaque and Chowdury 1998: 72) and is an alternative means of conceptualizing experiences (Gazi and Chowdhury 2003). Recently, body-mapping has been reported to reduce reliance on using Western biomedical terminology when asking questions about the female reproductive body (Cornwall 2002, Wallace et al. 2018, Kenny et al. 2019). Kenny et al. (2019) claim body-mapping to be the "best qualitative data collection method" for engaging young people in Cambodia on sexual and reproductive health issues because it reduces language and cultural barriers, but their young rural women had difficulty drawing and locating uteruses on body maps. Cornwall, who used body-mapping with rural illiterate women to explore women's understandings of anatomy and physiology in Zimbabwe, noted that "rural, non-literate women are not 'ignorant': they theorize and make sense of their experiences within frames of reference that are different from the biological model" (Cornwall 2002: 228). One aspect of Cornwall's approach that made much sense to me when I considered the use of clay sculpturing as a body-mapping medium with illiterate Nepalese women was that she gave the women sticks to draw in the earth before asking them to draw on paper, to address the women's initial resistance to body-mapping through drawing.

Yet, MacCormack's technique has not been universally regarded as successful by other researchers using it with women and children with low literacy (Zaman, Mustaque and Chowdhury 1998, Cornwall 2002, Gazi and Chowdhury 2003, Kesby and Gwanzura-Ottemöller 2007). In a very recent use of body-mapping in Indonesia with *belian* – traditional Indonesian midwives – to explore infertility, Bennett (2017: 114) noted: "I had expected the *belian* to engage in a practice that was for them culturally unfamiliar and required competencies that were outside of their comfort zone". She stated that body-mapping only made sense for these women "when it was literally performed on and through the body" (Bennett 2017: 115).

In Nepal, MacCormack's body-mapping technique has been used with small groups of women to study perceptions of HIV and sexually transmitted diseases (STDs) in a remote mountain community (Butcher and Kievelitz 1997). The researchers observed the women's resistance to it, which they discerned as a lack of confidence to draw. Like Cornwall (2002), they responded by giving the women sticks to draw in the earth before asking them to draw on paper (Butcher and Kievelitz 1997). This appeared to help. Sturley (2000) used a drawing-form body-mapping with mixed focus groups in another rural community in rural Nepal to explore men's vasectomy experiences. The villagers were illiterate and moreover "drawing is not practised as an art here" and there was a reluctance to draw on top of anyone else's line (Sturley 2000: 86). The participants also found the process embarrassing (Sturley 2000). She later thought that providing an outline of the entire body would have worked better than free drawing of body parts (Sturley 2000). Our own experience with Nepalese women, though, suggests that this may not be the case. Alison Morgan, a doctor who has used simple body-mapping techniques with rural women in Tansen, in the midwest district of Palpa, thinks that the use of body-mapping has limitations if women have limited understandings of the body (personal communication, 3 July 2014). Nirmala Prajapati, former national coordinator of United Nations Populations Fund-supported Youth Peer Nepal (Y-PEER Nepal), which delivers adolescent sexual and reproductive health (ASRH) education, thinks that body knowledge is not the only limitation to successful body-mapping. She believes that adolescents in Nepal find it difficult to draw and talk about external or internal (reproductive) body parts because of cultural taboos on discussing sexual and reproductive health issues in public (personal communication, 23 October 2014).

Yet body-mapping is clearly a powerful tool. A systematic review on body-mapping identifies it as having significant potential for global health interventions because it can be "used as an interdisciplinary research method across diverse cultures to address critical issues in health and is amenable to sharing information between researchers and the public" (Jager et al. 2016: 15). Boydell et al. (2020) agree. Indeed, it is these characteristics of body-mapping that make it necessary for global health research (Aboelela et al. 2007).

Using clay as a body-mapping medium

The reports of unsuccessful use of drawing-form body-mapping with low literacy populations led me to dismiss MacCormack's drawing technique for my proposed research with sex-trafficked women in Nepal. However, realizing the potential power of body-mapping as a communication medium, I reflected on the relationship the women of Nepal had with *mato* (clay or earth) for inspiration to design a new body-mapping form for our research. I had seen the connectedness of rural village women in the Annapurna region in midwest Nepal with the earth, for example, in cooking on a *chulo* (stove) made from the clay in the ground there (see Figure 3.1). (Note: there is no distinction between earth and clay in Nepal.)

I saw that clay is a culturally familiar material for Nepalese women. Clay is used in many Hindu religious rituals in Nepal. It is used to make *diyos* (oil lamps, which use cotton wicks dipped in ghee or oils), burned in many traditions and in temples to ask the gods to fulfill wishes during the Dashain, Tihar (Dipawali) and other festivals. Four weeks prior to the Rali Rali festival, unmarried girls in a Brahmin-Chettri (high caste)

Figure 3.1 A Nepali woman cooking on a *chulo* (clay stove) in the Annapurna
region in mid-west Nepal

Credit: Tricia Ong.

community in midwestern Nepal make clay images of the Hindu God
Shiva and his wife Parbati, who are then "married" to one another
on the opening day of the festival and subsequently washed down the
river (Bennett 2002). In a Tharu (indigenous) community living on the
plains that border India, clay is used as an altar and families "use clay
sculptures to represent the *duota*" (Maslak 2003: 156). *Duota* means
spirit. Clay, for the Tharu, embodies the spirits and gods (Maslak 2003).
Nepal's Newari ethnic group also has a hereditary occupational caste of
potters from Thimi (Foley 2013).

Apart from direct observation of clay use in the many and colourful
festivals in Nepal, I had also observed how Nepalese women naturally
work with it in three dimensions in a clay workshop that I cofacilitated
for an art therapy and women's reproductive health project with sex-
trafficked women (see Chapter 4). It seemed to me that these women of
Nepal – some of whom had low literacy levels – learned by "seeing" and
"doing", which I also observed with uneducated women in rural villages
of Nepal (see Ong, Mellor and Chettri 2020). However, in the workshop

mentioned earlier, clay enabled them to express their thoughts and knowledge in an authentic way and, sometimes, in non-verbal form.

Clay, then, became a focus for me in considering an alternate form to drawing in body-mapping for our proposed research. Using clay as a body-mapping medium was breaking new ground. Clay engages with the four senses of "sight, touch, sound and smell" (Malchiodi 2007). It connects to the body, so it is suitable for body-related work (Sherwood 2004, Elbrecht 2012). However, as with the tracing-form body-mapping, clay can elicit trauma and so ought to be used with professional expertise (Sherwood 2004, Elbrecht 2012). Australian clay therapist, Patricia Sherwood (2004: 3) illuminates how trauma elicitation can occur through clay:

> work in my clinical practice with clay demonstrates that the attraction of clay lies in its capacity to capture experience as it emerges in the immediacy of the moment from the client's body, and in the surprising and often powerfully evocative forms it arouses in the client's consciousness.

She also cautions therapists not to use clay with pregnant women (Sherwood 2004), though it is not clear why. She suggests working "thematically" or in a guided way to enable clients to remain focussed on immediate issues (Sherwood 2004). She also works with limited amounts of clay, whereas others work with "clay fields", which allows for a deeper immersion in clay that may trigger trauma more readily (Elbrecht 2012). Even so, I had observed trauma triggered through the limited use of clay with sex-trafficked women in Nepal.

Choosing photography to complement clay body-mapping

Visual tools within a PAR approach include the use of photographs and the act of taking them (i.e., photography). Reflecting on the early clay workshop I facilitated in Nepal, I saw how clay body-mapping could be improved with these methods. Photography has long been used as a research technique in anthropology and sociology, though it was only in the mid-1990s that Caroline Wang and Mary Ann Burris, from the USA, developed it as an accepted tool in health research. They used photography as a means of enabling women in Yunnan, China, to capture and reflect on their lives in relation to their reproductive health needs (Wang and Burris 1994, Wang, Burris and Ping 1996), later calling the technique "photovoice" (Wang and Burris 1997: 369).

Their method involves giving cameras to children, village women, grassroots community workers, and other people who have little control over decisions that affect their lives, to photograph aspects of their lives and so document it. This is in contrast to having their lives described by health specialists and policymakers or having professional photographers document it (Wang and Burris 1994). The photographs were then used for reflection on their needs, to promote dialogue, encourage action, and inform policy. Their method is underpinned by critical consciousness theory, feminist theory, and documentary photography (Wang and Burris 1994). A key point is that it is an approach that is accessible to anyone who can learn to use a camera and so is suitable for use with illiterate populations (Wang and Burris 1997). They believe that photovoice can reinforce the cleverness, originality, and inventiveness of society's most vulnerable populations (Wang and Burris 1997). They see it as being flexible and adaptable to specific participatory goals, for different groups and communities and for distinct public health issues.

I became interested in photovoice when I discovered its use in an isolated maternal health study in Nepal with women from marginalized populations with a "lack of verbal fluency" (Morrison et al. 2009: 27). However, I quickly recognized that photovoice was not suitable for our research, given that we hoped to capture personal reproductive body knowledge in a culture where discussing sexual and reproductive health is sensitive. It is clearly not culturally appropriate to ask the women to photograph their own reproductive bodies. Still, there was a related approach in a nascent form that remained largely undefined: photoethnography (Shuster 2009). I saw the potential to define it for our research. We could give cameras to the women to photograph the clay work of their reproductive bodies, and we would later use the photographs as the focus of reflection and discussion. The clay photographs could then become an "ethnography" of the women's bodies. This process would enable the women to photograph their clay work in any way they wished, and perhaps elicit what they might otherwise say without solely relying on words. I had already observed the power of photography in a reproductive health context with sex-trafficked women in Nepal, so I also knew of its potential (see Chapter 4).

The design of the Clay Embodiment Research Method

The methodological challenges of our proposed research with sex-trafficked women in Nepal relate to the cultural sensitivity of the research topic (sexuality and reproduction), the low literacy of the intended research participants, their possible reticence at being candid with us (researchers) because of the strong and unrelenting stigmatization they faced in their communities and society at large, and the limited time in which to complete our fieldwork (see Chapter 4). At the crossroad of deciding on final methods for our research, I was uncertain as to which methodological approach to take. I then realized that I did not need to decide between one or other – I could use all that I was interested in, synergistically, to produce more insightful data than any one method alone, and perhaps within a shorter timeframe. The method I proposed for our research, and one accepted by relevant ethics bodies, applied the lens of critical ethnography to active participant observation, and, within the inspirations of PAR, the visual methods of (clay) body-mapping with and photoethnography. These are the methodological roots of CERM. They, in turn, are underpinned by feminist theory – notably critical theory and standpoint theory. The findings emerging from the use of CERM would also be analyzed through the lens of the feminist theory of intersectionality, which is concerned with the intersections between forms or systems of oppression, domination, or discrimination (Crenshaw 1990, May 2015). As it applies to our proposed study in Nepal, the contextual perspective that feminist theory calls for was in large part established by, firstly, advice from Nepalese professionals (in particular Smriti Khadka of Asha Nepal and Nirmala Prajapati of Y-PEER Nepal) on sex trafficking, stigmatization, sexuality and reproduction, and Nepalese culture (see Chapter 2), and, secondly, the day-to-day input from my remarkable Nepalese research assistant, Sabrina Chettri. Similarly, CERM calls for empathy and trust between facilitators/researchers and participants to give effect to its lens of critical ethnography and visual methods used in PAR. In our case this would be fostered by the close involvement of our partner organizations in Nepal (Asha Nepal and CAP Nepal: see Chapters 4 and 7) and employing the aforementioned local female bilingual Nepali research assistant of similar age to our intended participants, and who would be present at all contact with them.

Conclusion

This chapter discusses the process of developing a feminist approach to sensitive research with one of the most stigmatized, oppressed, and marginalized women in Nepal – sex-trafficked women. It tackles the challenges of trying to find an approach that begins from the perspectives of the women. I explored critical ethnography and PAR, and their drawbacks in the context of our research, mainly that ethnography and PAR require long time periods in the field, the traditional PAR drawing technique of body-mapping had not been successful with illiterate populations in rural Nepal, and PAR techniques of photography needed to be adapted to ensure cultural sensitivity in relation to its approach to discussion of sexual and reproductive health issues. The approach I designed is CERM, comprising the critical ethnographic technique of active participant observation and two PAR methods – a new method of body-mapping using clay and photoethnography. Primarily, clay underpins the method as a familiar material for Nepalese women. The next chapter focuses on the development and implementation of CERM with our vulnerable population of young Low literate sex-trafficked women in Nepal.

Note

1 Body-mapping has been used in other contexts. However, for the purposes of this book, we will focus on the sexual and reproductive health context.

References

Aboelela, S. et al. 2007. Defining interdisciplinary research: conclusions from a critical review of the literature. *Health Services Research*, 42(11), 329–46.

Bennett, L. 2002. *Dangerous wives and sacred sisters: social and symbolic roles of high-caste women in Nepal*. 2nd ed. Kathmandu: Mandala Publications.

Bennett, L.R. 2017. Indigenous healing knowledge and infertility in Indonesia: Learning about cultural safety from Sasak midwives. *Medical Anthropology*, 36(2), 111–24.

Boydell, K. et al. 2020. Applying body-mapping to research with marginalised and vulnerable groups. In: K. Boydell, ed., *Applying body-mapping in research: an arts-based method*. New York: Routledge, 6–17.

Boyle, M. 2012. *Research in action: a guide to Participatory Action Research (Research Report)*. Canberra: Department of Social Services. https://www.dss.gov.au/sites/default/files/documents/06_2012/research_in_action.pdf [Accessed 6 May 2022].

Butcher, K. and Kievelitz, U. 1997. Planning with PRA: HIV and STD in a Nepalese mountain community. *Health and Policy Planning*, 12(3), 253–61.

Cameron, M. 1998. *On the edge of the auspicious: gender and caste in Nepal*. Kathmandu: Mandala Publications.

Cornwall, A. 2002. Body-mapping: bridging the gap between biomedical messages, popular knowledge and lived experience. In: A. Cornwall and A. Welbourn, eds, *Realising rights: transforming approaches to sexual and reproductive wellbeing*. London: Zed Books, 217–31.

Cornwall, A. and Jewkes, R. 1995. What is participatory research? *Social Sciences and Medicine*, 41(12), 1667–76.

Crenshaw, K. 1990. Mapping the margins: intersectionality, identity politics, and violence against women of color. *Stanford Law Review*, 43(6), 1241–99.

De Laine, M. 1997. *Ethnography: theory and applications in health research.* Sydney: Maclennan and Petty.

DeWalt, K. and DeWalt, B. 2011. *Participant observation: a guide for fieldworkers.* Blue Ridge Summit: AltaMira Press.

Elbrecht, C. 2012. *Trauma healing at the clay field: a sensorimotor art therapy approach.* London: Jessica Kingsley Publishers.

Foley, B. 2013. *The social lives of pots and potters in the Kathmandu Valley.* School for International Training. https://digitalcollections.sit.edu/cgi/viewcontent.cgi?article=2766&context=isp_collection [Accessed 21 April 2022].

Gazi, R. and Chowdhury, A. 2003. Perceptions of rural Bangladeshi women on sexually transmitted infections. *South Asian Anthropologist*, 3(2), 177–90.

Handwerker, W. 2001. *Quick ethnography: a guide to rapid multi-methods.* Walnut Creek: Alta Mira Press.

Harding, S. 1993. Rethinking standpoint epistemology: what is strong objectivity?. In: L. Alcoff and E. Potter, eds, *Feminist Epistemologies*. New York/London: Routledge.

Harding, S,. ed. 2004. *The Feminist Standpoint Theory Reader*. New York and London: Routledge.

Hartsock, N.C.M. 1983. The feminist standpoint: developing the ground for a specifically feminist historical materialism. In: S. Harding and M.B. Hintikka, eds, *Discovering reality: feminist perspectives on epistemology, metaphysics, methodology, and philosophy of science*. Dordrecht: Kluwer Academic Publishers, 283–311.

Hesse-Biber, S.N., ed. 2014. A re-invitation to feminist research. In: S. Hesse-Biber, ed., *Feminist Research Practice: A Primer*. Thousand Oaks: Sage, 1–13.

Hesse-Biber, S.N., Leavy, P. and Yaiser, M.L., 2004. Feminist approaches to research as a process: Reconceptualizing epistemology, methodology, and method. In: S.N. Hesse-Biber and M.L. Yaiser, eds., *Feminist Perspectives on Social Research,* New York: Oxford University Press, 3–26.

Hussain, B. and Asad, A.Z. 2012. A critique on feminist research methodology. *Journal of Politics and Law*, 5(4), 202–7.

Jager, A. et al. 2016. Embodied ways of storytelling the self: a systematic review of body-mapping. *Forum: Qualitative Social Research*, 17(2). http://www.qualitative-research.net/index.php/fqs/article/view/2526/3986 [Accessed 24 April 2022].

Jorgensen, D. 1989. *Participant observation: a methodology for human studies.* Newbury Park: SAGE.

Kenny, B. et al. 2019. A qualitative exploration of the sexual and reproductive health knowledge of adolescent mothers from indigenous populations in Ratanak Kiri Province, Cambodia. *Rural and Remote Health*, 19(4), 2540.

Kesby, M. and Gwanzura-Ottemöller, F. 2007. Researching sexual health: two participatory action research projects in Zimbabwe. In: S. Kindon, R. Pain and M. Kesby, eds, *Participatory action research approaches and methods: connecting people, participation and place*. London: Routledge, 71–9.

Kindon, S., Pain, R. and Kesby, M. 2007. Participatory action research approaches and methods. *Connecting People, Participation and Place*. Abingdon: Routledge.

Kramer, M.W. and Adams, T.E. 2017. *Ethnography*. In: M. Allen, ed., *The SAGE Encyclopedia of Communication Research Methods*. Thousand Oaks: SAGE, 458–61. https://methods.sagepub.com/reference/the-sage-encyclope dia-of-communication-research-methods [Accessed 24 April 2022].

Leavy, P. (2017). *Research design: quantitative, qualitative, mixed Methods, arts-based, and community-based participatory research approaches*. New York: The Guilford Press.

Leavy, P. and Harris, A. 2018. *Contemporary feminist research from theory to practice*. New York: Guilford Press.

MacCormack, C. 1985. Lay concepts affecting utilisation of family planning services in Jamaica. *Journal of Tropical Medicine and Hygiene*, 88(4), 281–5.

Malchiodi, C. 2007. *Art therapy sourcebook*. New York: McGraw-Hill.

Maslak, M. 2003. *Daughters of the Tharu: gender, ethnicity, religion, and the education of Nepali girls*. New York: Routledge-Falmer.

May, V. 2015. *Pursuing intersectionality, unsettling dominant imaginaries*. New York: Routledge.

Morrison, J. et al. 2010. Understanding how women's groups improve maternal and newborn health in Makwanpur, Nepal: a qualitative study. *International Health*, 2(1), 25–35.

Norlander, S. 2017. *Critical ethnography*. In M. Allen, ed., *The SAGE Encyclopedia of Communication Research Methods*. Thousand Oaks: SAGE, 458–60. https://methods.sagepub.com/reference/the-sage-encyclopedia-of-communication-research-methods [Accessed 24 April 2022].

Ong, P. 2018. *Reproductive health for the marginalised: knowledge of young women trafficked into the sex industry in Nepal*. Thesis (PhD). Deakin University.

Ong T., Mellor, D. and Chettri, S. 2019. Multiplicity of stigma: the experiences, fears and knowledge of young trafficked women in Nepal. Sexual and Reproductive Health Matters, 27(3), 32–48. https://www.tandfonline.com/doi/full/10.1080/26410397.2019.1679968 [Accessed 12 March 2022].

Ong, T., Mellor, D. and Chettri, S. 2020. Clay as a medium in three-dimensional body-mapping. *Forum: Qualitative Social Research*, 21(2), art.9. https://www.qualitative-research.net/index.php/fqs/article/download/3380/4567?inl ine=1 [Accessed 12 March 2022].

Ong, T., Mellor, D. and Chettri, S. 2021. "Females are always dominated and disregarded by males, just because they are female": the continuation of patriarchal norms for young trafficked women in Nepal. *Culture, Health and Sexuality*, 1–16.

Orchard, T. 2017. *Remembering the body: ethical issues in body-mapping research*. New York: Springer International Publishing.

Pain, R. et al. 2011. *Participatory action research toolkit: An introduction to using PAR as an approach to learning, research and action*. Durham: Durham University. http://communitylearningpartnership.org/wp-content/uploads/2017/01/PARtoolkit.pdf [Accessed 31 May 2022].

Palmer, D. and Caldas, B. 2016. Critical ethnography. In: K. King, Y.J. Lai and S. May, eds, *Research Methods in Language and Education. Encyclopedia of Language and Education*. Cham: Springer, 381–92. https://link.springer.com/referenceworkentry/10.1007/978-3-319-02329-8_28-1 [Accessed 31 May 2022].

Patton, M.Q. 2008. *Utilization-focused evaluation*. 4th ed. London: Sage.

Pelto, P. 2013. *Applied ethnography: guidelines for field research*. Abingdon: Routledge.

Pink, S. 2009. *Doing sensory ethnography*. Los Angeles: Sage.

Schubotz, D. 2019. *Participatory action research*. In: P. Atkinson et al., eds, *SAGE Research Method Foundations*. London: SAGE. https://methods.sagepub.com/foundations/participatory-action-research [Accessed on 31 May 2022].

Seppälä, T. 2020. Participatory photography with women's rights' activists in Nepal: towards a practice of decolonial solidarity. *In:* T. Seppälä, M, Sarantou and S. Miettinen, eds, *Arts-Based Methods for Decolonising Participatory Research*. New York: Routledge, 81–98.

Seppälä, T., Sarantou, M. and Miettinen, S. 2021. *Arts-Based Methods for Decolonising Participatory Research*. New York: Routledge.

Sherwood, P. 2004. *Healing art of clay therapy*. Camberwell: Australian Council for Educational Research.

Shuster, S. 2009. Resolving feminist dilemmas within ethnography: a case for photoethnography. *Annual meeting of the American Sociological Association Annual Meeting*, 8–11 August 2009, San Francisco.

Solomon, J. 2007. *Living with X: A body-mapping journey in the time of HIV/AIDS: a facilitator's guide*. Johannesburg: Regional Psychosocial Support Initiative.

Solomon, J. 2020. Foreword. In: K. Boydell, ed., *Applying body-mapping in research: an arts-based method*. New York: Routledge, xvi–xx.

Stevens, M. and Le Roux, N. 2011. A human rights violation: the forced sterilisation of HIV positive women. *Nursing Update*, 35(3), 32–5.

Sturley, A. 2000. *Mapping the effects of vasectomy., PLA Note 37: Special Issue: Sexual and Reproductive Health*. Holborn: International Institute for Environment and Development, 17, 83–86. http://pubs.iied.org/pdfs/6335IIED.pdf [Accessed 21 April 2022].

Thomas, J. 1993. *Doing critical ethnography*. Newbury Park: Sage.

Thomas, J. and O'Maolchatha, A. 1989. Reassessing the critical metaphor: an optimistic revisionist view. *Justice Quarterly*, 6(2), 143–72.

Triandis, H.C. 2018. *Individualism and collectivism*. New York: Routledge.

Van Maanen, J. 2011. *Tales of the field: On writing ethnography.* 2nd ed. Chicago: University of Chicago Press.

Wallace, H. et al. 2018. Body-mapping to explore reproductive ethno-physiological beliefs and knowledge of contraception in Timor-Leste. *Qualitative Health Research*, 28(7), 1171–84.

Wang, C. and Burris, M. 1994. Empowerment through photo novella: portraits of participation. *Health Education Quarterly*, 21(2), 171–86. http://citeseerx.ist.psu.edu/viewdoc/download?doi=10.1.1.906.6918&rep=rep1&type=pdf/ [Accessed 20 April 2022].

Wang, C., Burris, M. and Ping, X. 1996. Chinese village women as visual anthropologists: a participatory approach to reaching policymakers. *Social Science & Medicine*, 42(10), 1391–400.

Wang, C. and Burris, M. 1997. Photovoice: concept, methodology, and use for participatory needs assessment. *Health, Education and Behaviour*, 24(3), 369–87. https://deepblue.lib.umich.edu/bitstream/handle/2027.42/67790/10.1177_109019819702400309.pdf?sequence=2 [Accessed 20 April 2022].

Zaman, S., Mustaque, A. and Chowdhury, A. 1998. Exploring women's perceptions of reproduction through body-mapping: a research note from Bangladesh. *Medische Antropologie*, 10(1), 69–75.

4 The development and implementation of the Clay Embodiment Research Method

Introduction

CERM is new. It comprises clay, body-mapping, and photography, and is underpinned by the feminist research methods and feminist theory (Chapter 3). We found it to be "culturally sensitive" and a particularly powerful tool in research and education when working with populations with low literacy. This chapter explores CERM's early and current design and use. Part 1 looks at our early exploration in using clay in body-mapping and the lessons that led to the current CERM design. Part 2 discusses the implementation of the current CERM model as implemented in our five-month fieldwork with six young women (aged 14–22 years) with low literacy who had been trafficked into the sex industry in Nepal.

Part 1: Discovering clay and photography for sex-trafficked women in Nepal

Early clay and photography workshops with sex-trafficked women in Nepal

In 2011, I was invited to work on an art therapy and women's reproductive health project with sex-trafficked women in Nepal with Art2Healing, an Australian not-for-profit organization that provides trauma recovery and mental health specialized care for women and children who have experienced gender-based violence and sex trafficking (Art2Healing 2017). At the time, I was working as a creative arts therapist specializing in women's reproductive health in Australia. On the project, I cofacilitated two workshops with the women – one on clay work and the other on photography. The (approximate) 15 women were mostly young (under 30 years) and had been through varying degrees of

DOI: 10.4324/b23275-4

trauma related to being sex trafficked. In the clay workshop, the women sat on cushions around a red sāri laid on the floor. Each was given a hand-sized ball of clay on a piece of cardboard and asked to create a self-image with it. We played soft music in the background. Some of the women puzzled over experimenting with the clay, making three-dimensional sculptures of themselves. Some had no hesitation over what they wanted to create. For others this took some time. I was struck by how naturally these Nepalese women worked with the clay once they started, how very absorbed and calm they were. In contrast, floodgates opened in the session afterwards reflecting on their clay work. The women shared stories about themselves with much emotional intensity. We, as art therapists, had to work hard to hold the space and keep it safe for the women. At the end of the workshop, some women wanted to keep their clay work. Others quickly destroyed theirs. We had a mess to clean up as the wet clay disintegrated the cardboard and left clay debris all over the floor.

At the photography workshop, I brought photographs (laminated in A4 size) of, among others, my family (husband, daughter, and son), my daughter playing as a child, and me in labour in the delivery suite of an Australian hospital. These were used to prompt discussion on women's reproductive health issues. The room exploded with chatter about menstruation, pregnancy and birthing, and sexual intercourse, all from the Nepalese perspective. The women were also curious about my Australian family. Not knowing then about the Nepali cultural taboos at the time on talking about women's reproductive health matters, I was surprised at how little anatomical and biological knowledge the women had. Even the women who had given birth had little idea of its bio-logical processes. Still, I felt comfortable with the conversation and even shared my personal experiences of endometriosis and adenomyosis, and how this had led me to working in the women's reproductive health field. In this session, I was struck by the candidness of the women, the laughter we shared, and the power of photography to open such a rich dynamic discussion about sensitive issues.

About a year after the project, Smriti Khadka, the manager of Asha Nepal, which works with girls who have been sex trafficked and sexually abused (see Asha Nepal 2021), whom I met on the project, invited me to run a reproductive health workshop with adolescent girls at Asha Nepal, and later to develop a training manual. This was the beginning of an ongoing relationship with her and Asha Nepal, and the enormous support they gave to my subsequent research with sex-trafficked women. Just prior to my fieldwork for that research, she asked me to run two exploratory clay workshops with small groups of sexually abused girls and the staff counsellor at one of Asha Nepal's homes. In these workshops, we similarly made a circle of the floor, gave the girls hand-sized balls of clay, and asked them to create whatever they wished. Spontaneously, the girls made amazing three-dimensional clay sculptures, capturing different aspects of their lives in their rural villages of origin. During clay-making the girls were calm and quiet, though a little chatter went backwards and forwards between them. They seemed to be enjoying the process. In the reflection session, they described their clay work and told stories about life – with their families, in their rural villages, and more. One of the girls made a beautiful temple and told us about missing her mother, tears running down her cheeks. Another revealed abuse in a domestic labour context. Yet another told a story about a negative experience with the Nepalese police.

In one of the workshops, the staff counsellor caught my eye across the room and indicated that she was shocked by the revelations. She later told me that the girls had never shared these stories, and she had learned things about them that she had not known before. I, on the other hand, was surprised that the girls shared these things with me as I was an outsider to the culture and barely knew the girls. I also recognized that we had, unintentionally, entered a therapeutic space and working with clay had been cathartic. I was wracked with guilt. I thanked the girls; it was an emotional moment. This was a warning about the power of clay, the care we needed to take not to enter a therapeutic space in my research, and how we would manage this with sex-trafficked women. This was an ethical issue as my research was not intended to be therapeutic.

Advice from Nepali women about clay body-mapping in research

When I was developing methods for my research, the first Nepalese person I consulted with was the aforementioned Smriti Khadka of Asha Nepal. I always found her kind and caring, and I believe she came to trust me as a professional and friend. This led to me suggesting that Asha Nepal become the organizational partner for my research (see Chapter 1). In this early conversation about the research, Smriti said that we should not use surveys. Like me, she wanted to ensure the voices of the girls were "heard" in the research and that the experience would be "educative" and "empowering" for them. I mentioned that I had been thinking of using clay as a new body-mapping method (see Chapter 3) and that the idea had come from the clay workshop with Art2Healing. Smriti was highly supportive and encouraged me to use a participatory approach – grouping women who had had similar trafficking experiences together – because the women and girls would more likely share in groups. It also respected and worked with the Nepalese collectivist culture.

I also discussed my ideas for clay body-mapping with Nirmala Prajapati, former national coordinator of the United Nations Population Fund (UNFPA), supported Youth-Peer Nepal (Y-PEER Nepal). She was introduced to me by ASRH staff at UNFPA after a meeting with Catherine Kamkong Breen, former deputy representative of UNFPA in Nepal, who herself had encouraged me to use arts-based methods in my research on hearing about my background in creative arts therapy. I talked about a thematic approach to clay body-mapping and Nirmala suggested using simple reproductive body themes because of the sex-trafficked women's (likely) limited reproductive body knowledge. She also recommended working at a slow pace to ease gently into discussing culturally sensitive topics. Like Smriti, she also suggested a participatory (group) approach. Nirmala was very supportive of the research overall and showed me some of the participatory work of Y-PEER through their Facebook page. They were also using some unique three-dimensional approaches to ASRH education.

Photography and clay body-mapping

As mentioned, we saw how effective photography was in eliciting story-telling at the Art2Healing photography workshop – using women's photographs of their clay works within a group was yet personal and intimate and can reveal much about their reproductive health knowledge. Still, I was cautious that, like clay body-mapping, it may trigger suppressed memories of trauma. Photography has been reported to be powerful and therapeutic when used in a pain study and not just with research participants (Bendelow 1993) and it has only had limited use in maternal health research and limited use in Nepal generally at the time (see Chapter 3).

Scoping the Clay Embodiment Research Method

The years-long consideration of theory, practice, and feedback finally produced the methodology for my PhD research, incorporating clay and photography. To be descriptive, I called it Clay Embodiment Research Method (CERM). Its key elements are active participant observation, a series of participatory thematic clay body-mapping workshops, and a group interview using photographs (of the clay work from the clay body-mapping workshops) (see Chapter 3). The clay body-mapping workshops and group interview would be guided by a set of flexible questions. The size of the groups in our clay body-mapping workshops would be limited to four because of the sensitivity of the research. This was guided by what other researchers had done in focus groups on a menstruation study in Nepal (see Crawford, Menger and Kaufman 2014). How clay and photography affected the women was yet to be known, so keeping the groups small was very important.

Part 2: Implementing the Clay Embodiment Research Method with young sex-trafficked women in Nepal

Having received all ethics approvals for implementing my proposed CERM in Nepal, we started its implementation in December 2015, and completed the last designated workshop four months later. The preparation of the raw data (transcription and translation) took an extra month to complete.

For me as researcher, this fieldwork component of my PhD research project involving research participants felt it had three distinct experiences: a pilot of how the CERM workshops would work with young Nepalese women (not being any of the actual research participants); an "entrée to the field" of getting to know the women invited to participate in the CERM workshops and the context of how they lived (this being the first of CERM's components); and the actual CERM workshops and group discussion (the second and third of CERM's components). It seems likely to me that this will also be the experience of others in adapting the CERM approach for research or educational purposes.

On-the-ground piloting of the CERM workshop approach with young Nepalese women

I had set out to run two CERM-based clay body-mapping workshops with young women in Nepal before applying the full CERM with our actual research participants. My intention was to observe the extent to which it worked for the women and find out what might need to be improved before using it with the research participants. As it turned out, I proceeded with only one of the two intended "pilot" workshops, and this in itself is a story worth relating as an illumination of how much reliance there is on local networks of relationships to get things organized (or not) in Nepal and, I am sure, in other places where CERM can be a particularly effective tool.

The first of these workshops was held at the Mahendra Vidhya Ashram school in Barahisthan, 13 kilometres east of Kathmandu, with four young women, with my research assistant, Sabrina Chettri, a young single Nepali woman (see Chapter 7). Both the location and women were set up by Saru Shilpakar, a Y-PEER Nepal educator introduced to us by the previously mentioned Nirmala. Saru was able to get access to the art room at the school for the workshop because she was a former pupil and knew the principal well. She recruited four women as workshop participants (only three turned up on the day) from the Bhaktapur Youth Information Forum (BYIF), which runs reproductive health workshops for young people in Bhaktapur, and where she is a volunteer. All women had some reproductive health education through BYIF and some through the school curriculum. Two of women were 18 years old from a Newari ethnic group, and had just finished high school. The other woman was from a Tamang ethnic group, aged 23, had never been to school, and ran a shop.

The second proposed pilot workshop was organized by another of Nirmala's contacts, Kamal Kafle, previously a communications coordinator for Y-PEER Nepal. The participants of this workshop were to have been girls at a high school in Kathmandu. However, in the time we had, we were not able to meet all the challenges this presented, notably gaining permission from a male school principal and addressing possible objections from parents given the sensitivity of reproductive health issues in Nepalese culture.

For the one-day pilot workshop, Sabrina and I picked the theme that we thought the women would most struggle with, as Sabrina did in her training: menstruation. For Sabrina, the challenge ("I need to think about this") was to create a representation in clay of an internal, hence unseen, body part. In the end, she created a uterus sliced open with blood within. It was detailed and beautifully touching. We thought that the women may similarly struggle, and we wanted to see how they might resolve this, and what might help them work it out for themselves.

At the workshop we put cushions in a circle on the floor, one for each woman and for Sabrina, Saru, and me. In front of each cushion, we placed a hand-sized ball of clay on a plastic mat and a *diyo* (clay vessel used in religious rituals) to water the clay if it dried out upon use. Sabrina and I faced one another in the circle so that we had an unobscured view of the women and their clay work.

At the start of the workshop, we gave the women simple instructions to create anything they knew about menstruation in clay. At first, the women could not think of a way to represent menstruation in clay. Eventually, however, the younger (and better educated) Newari women created representations of uteruses and menstrual pads with menstrual blood, perhaps recalling pictures from a book. The Tamang woman kept gazing at the ball of clay in her hands. To encourage her along, I gave Sabrina a pre-planned signal for us to work on our own clay balls. Saru, sitting next to her for a short time in the workshop, chatted to her (in Nepali), attempting to help her elicit her thoughts. Saru had to leave, but she then began to talk about the (Hindu) menstruation traditions she had practiced in her village community at menarche. She was Buddhist, so the harshness of the practices was surprising to Sabrina and me. The Newari women then shared their experiences, including that these once harmful practices were now celebrated as positive rituals for entering womanhood in their communities. We also spent a little time reflecting

Figure 4.1 Completed clay work on menstruation at the pilot of the Clay Embodiment Research Method in the art room of the Mahendra Vidhya Ashram school, Barahisthan, Bhaktapur

Credit: Tricia Ong.

on pregnancy in clay, even though none of the women had been pregnant or given birth. Unfortunately, the Tamang woman then wanted to leave, possibly because she was losing income from her shop (see also Ong, Mellor and Chettri 2020) (see Figure 4.1).

After lunch, we talked with the Newari women about their clay body-mapping experience. Nirmala joined us and offered insights into the women's clay work. After the Newari women left, she noticed that Sabrina had made a clay model of the uterus with an anatomical inaccuracy. Sabrina was puzzled as to what was inaccurate. Nirmala corrected it by remoulding her clay work, which got Sabrina excited that she had just discovered something new about the female reproductive body. We talked about the workshop, and noted that the women had created menstruation and pregnancy as an outer body experience. We reflected on the Tamang woman's early resistance to engage in clay making. Like the Newari women, she told us later she just did not know what to create. We felt that a menstruation theme – dealing with a body function that is largely invisible and a culturally sensitive topic – may have been confronting, and perhaps was not helped by a sense of feeling pressured to make something. Sabrina brilliantly came up with what I believe is an essential step in CERM: that we have a familiarization workshop – adding to the series of six we had planned – so the research participants could familiarize themselves with clay, and conceptualize being a girl. After seeking approval from Deakin University's Human Research Ethics Committee (DUHREC), we amended our CERM plan by including a seventh workshop: Workshop 1: "I am a women/girl" (see Figure 4.5).

Entrée to the field – recruiting and getting to know the trafficked women and girls (active participant observation)

Almost as soon as I arrived in Nepal, I immersed myself in the daily lives of the women and girls at Asha Nepal from whom we hoped to draw our research participants for the main study. At the Skills, Education and Empowerment (SEE) girls' hostel, I saw their daily routines where they lived, and quickly realized that our work with them had to fit in between domestic chores and school. Sometimes the girls got up at 4 a.m. to do homework before an early school start at 6.30 a.m. They would be home by lunchtime to help cook, do washing, and other chores. Then there was a similar afternoon and evening routine. The girls would often be exhausted at the end of their day. Nevertheless, in bright spirits they made time to have many lovely chats with us – about life and what interested them – on the sunny Asha Nepal rooftop, in the kitchen, and in the sunroom of their hostel. They would practise the

English they were learning at school, and I would practise my Nepali in turn. This was a great ice-breaker, as we would laugh at each other's incorrect pronunciations. The girls also sang and danced for us. We started to gain their trust.

Sabrina and I also ran clay workshops for the staff and girls at the SEE hostel to introduce the idea of clay body-mapping. These were fun for everyone, and we were amazed at the three-dimensional sculptures created. During one of these workshops, CERM inherited its Nepali name *mato ko khel* (play with clay). We took photographs of all the clay work and introduced the photography process. We recorded some singing by both staff and girls, and played it back to them as a way of showing how the conversations in the workshops and later interview would be recorded and transcribed.

This led to four young women from Asha Nepal participating in the research: Niuresha, Rosina, Soniya, and Sulob (see Chapter 1). From the study's perspective, they were the group of four unmarried trafficked women. We spent more time at Asha Nepal, answering questions they had about their participation, and just generally chatting. For them, we ran the CERM workshops and interview at Asha Nepal's counselling room in its main house. Smriti reached out to some other anti-trafficking organizations in Nepal for willing participants, but discovered these had strict gatekeeping to protect their young women and girls from being "over researched". After this, we decided to invoke the contingency of the research plan to increase the age range of participants from 13–18 years to 13–22 years (see Chapter 5). Smriti then found two other young women over the age of 18 from Asha Nepal's greater community of beneficiaries, who were working and studying and interested in participating in our research. However, it soon became clear that they were busy, and the workshop timeline clashed with their school exam schedule. Therefore, they decided to prioritize their education and chose not to participate. We were disappointed, but fully supported their decision. We ran a fun clay workshop purely for enjoyment. Then CAP Nepal expressed interest because their staff knew me from the therapeutic work with Art2Healing. We ran some clay workshops on the rooftop of the CAP Nepal home for their staff and the women and girls in their care, emphasizing the difference between therapy and research. From these Aisha and Indira expressed an interest in participating in the research. Two other women who were interested later told staff that they had returned to work in the sex industry, so no longer meet our entry criteria. From the study's perspective, Aisha and Indira formed the group of two married women, and for them we ran the CERM workshops and interview at CAP Nepal's home.

All six women consented to participate in the research using verbal, visual, and audio methods and "thumbprints" as a requirement of the Nepal Health Research Council (NHRC) (see Chapter 5).

Reception to clay use

In all the clay workshops that we ran for staff and women of Asha Nepal and CAP Nepal, it became very apparent that clay really was a culturally familiar material in Nepal, not just for women: men, women, and children enjoyed engaging with clay. The striking aspect was how naturally they used it in in three dimensions, that is, not as a medium for drawing lines of a diagram, but as sculptures of detail they laboured to produce. We can say that, in Nepal, we found little resistance to using clay for our purposes beyond initial frustrations of deciding what to represent. One of the most delightful moments with clay happened outside of our research when two girls from Asha Nepal went out to the garden at the SEE hostel, dug up some earth, and made sculptures of local animals, which they were bursting to show Sabrina and me on a visit. Some of the staff at Asha Nepal, who were not able to participate in workshops, also told us they had used clay as children. By the way they described the experience, it seemed reverential. Given that clay is used in religious rituals, this was not really a surprise (see Chapter 3).

The themed participatory clay body-mapping workshops

The clay body-mapping workshops we ran lasted between 45 and 60 minutes, mostly a week apart. They were on a Saturday, a non-school day, for the girls from Asha Nepal, and at time negotiated with them. Workshops for the women from CAP Nepal were also scheduled to suit them, given that they lived in the community and had to commute by public bus with their infants to get to CAP Nepal.

Each of the seven workshops of our CERM plan had a focal theme as described below. I have included some examples of clay work the women produced and snippets of what the women said, to illustrate their responses to the different themes of the workshops. I have also repeatedly noted the ethnicity, age, and marital status of the women to provide more context to each discussion point.

Workshop 1: I am a woman/girl

In the first workshop, the women were asked to use the hand-sized balls of clay given to each of them to create anything that represented for them what it means to be a woman or girl quite generally. This was to be the familiarization workshop that Sabrina had suggested after our pilot workshops. The women were initially hesitant, so Sabrina and I joined in, playing with our own clay balls, and this seemed to have encouraged the women's own creativity with the malleable material in their hands.

One of the more striking clay creations was Aisha's (a Chettri, 20, married with one daughter) creation of three sculptures, one of herself as a girl, one of her husband and her, and one of her as she was then, made during the workshop with Indira. She explained that they depicted her biological development from a girl to becoming a woman in Nepali culture: "This is from my childhood, where I reached adolescence and my boobs started coming. This is after I got pregnant with my daughter, and this is my husband's picture." The clay representation of her husband is with an erect penis (see Figure 4.2). When staff at the premises

Figure 4.2 Aisha's clay sculpture of her naked husband with an erect penis
Credit: Tricia Ong.

(CAP Nepal) unintentionally interrupted us by walking into our room, Aisha threw her body over the clay work to cover it up. It was an immediate lesson for us to make available a piece of cloth in our tool kit for the women to cover up their clay work in the workshops should they wish.

Workshop 2: Outer female reproductive body

The aim of Workshop 2 was for the women to produce their conceptualization of the outer female reproductive body parts. The women mostly created clay works of breasts and buttocks. Some made what they called "vaginas" – the common expression for any and all lower female reproductive parts in Nepal. Rosina (a Magar girl, 14, unmarried) forgot about a "vagina" and later moulded one from clay and added it to her sculpture. Soniya (a Brahmin, 18, unmarried) refused to make a "visible" "vagina" and, when describing her clay work, said: "I have not made the front one". None of the women would use the Nepali word for vagina (*yoni*). They referred to it as "the place where we pee".

At the end of the workshop at Asha Nepal with Niuresha, Rosina, Soniya, and Sulob, Niuresha (a Tamang, 17, unmarried) wrote the word *puti* in watery clay residue on a clay mat, and then quickly destroyed it. All the women saw it other than me. Sulob (a Tamang, 18, unmarried) said the word *puti* is a "dirty word" for "vagina". Sabrina then said *puti* out loud. Niuresha and Sulob both agreed that it is a dirty word. Rosina, Niuresha, and Sulob continued to discuss this, hiding their embarrassment with moments of laughter. Soniya did not engage in the discussion. However, this incident was the turning point in developing group cohesion with this group of girls. It was clear that they felt the workshop was a safe space to talk about culturally sensitive issues, and it seemed clear that they had begun to trust each other and us.

Workshop 3: Inner female reproductive body

The aim of Workshop 3 was for the women to produce their conceptualization of the inner female reproductive body parts, such as vagina, uterus, ovaries, fallopian tubes, etc. Compared to the earlier workshops, the women and girls found this difficult. In the Asha Nepal workshop with Niuresha, Rosina, Soniya, and Sulob, the women used the clay to mimic diagrams that one might see in a health textbook. We had earlier seen the girls look at nurse's health text in the sunroom at Asha Nepal's SEE hostel so surmised a connection (see Figure 4.3).

In the CAP Nepal workshop with Aisha and Indira, Aisha (a Chettri, 20, married with one daughter) copied Indira's (a Magar, 22, married

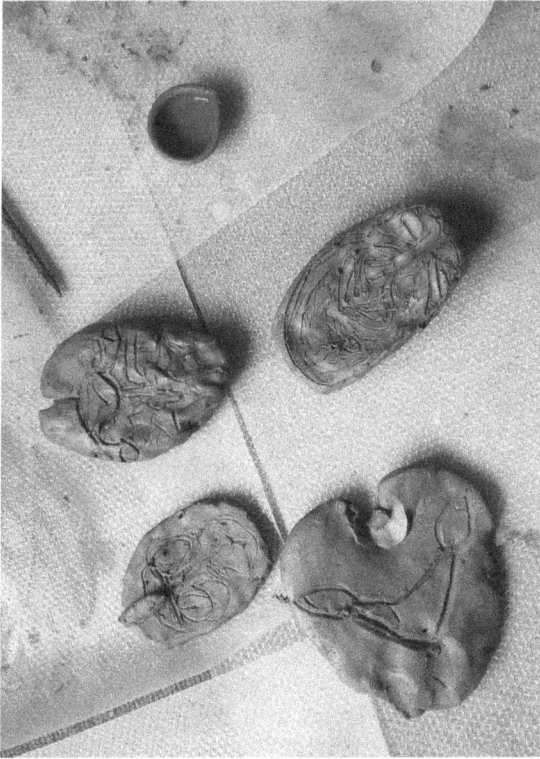

Figure 4.3 Two-dimensional clay work of the inner female reproductive body as it might appear in health textbooks by Niuresha, Soniya, Rosina, and Sulob (from top left and clockwise)

Credit: Tricia Ong.

with a son) anatomically incorrect uterus, because she had no concept of what these inner body parts looked like. Sabrina used Indira's clay sculpture to guide a conversation about the length of the vaginal canal at birth. Indira then said she had idea: "It's 1 or 2 palm widths" refer-ring (as it turned out) to a male doctor's hand. Aisha then proceeded to tell us that she also knew something about its length from giving birth: "It's probably wide. I have never seen it...How wide or how big is prob-ably what a doctor knows. They do operation every day. They should know...You can't see anything when you give birth." The sharing of their experiential knowledge of the vaginal canal facilitated by Indira's clay work continued for some time, and the women seemed to be comfortable sharing their knowledge.

Workshop 4: Menstruation

The aim of Workshop 4 was for the women to produce their conceptualization of the process of menstruation and the menstrual cycle.

All the women created clay sculptures of themselves menstruating as experiencing abdominal pain, changing sensations in the vaginal area, and having pimples. Sulob (a Tamang, 18, unmarried) created pads with menstrual blood on them. When we asked about the age at which they first menstruated, all of them shared experiences and knowledge of Hindu menstruation traditions, some of which have the effect of making women untouchable at menstruation – *chaupadi* (Aisha/Soniya), *gupha* and *guniyo cholo* (Indira) (see Chapter 2 for information on these Hindu menstruation traditions). They include seclusion, touch, and sight restrictions related to the kitchen and people (men and women), and not being able to participate in religious rituals (Niuresha, Rosina, Sulob). Some of women were not aware they had practised any. Soniya (a Brahmin,18, unmarried) shocked Niuresha (a Tamang, 17, unmarried) with her community's harsh practice of Hindu menstruation traditions. Niuresha was from a Buddhist community, and believed "if our hearts are clean, we can touch anything" (see also Ong, Mellor and Chettri 2019).

Like the pilot workshops, menstruation was represented as an outer body experience in clay. None of women created anything to do with menstruation traditions in clay, but the women's clay work facilitated a dynamic discussion about them.

Workshop 5: Pregnancy

The aim of Workshop 5 was for the women to produce their conceptualization of pregnancy and childbirth.

The women and girls created sculptures of women as pregnant or giving birth. All the women knew something about pregnancy and childbirth from either giving birth (Aisha and Indira), from having seen "sisters-in-law" giving birth (Soniya), cows giving birth in the village (Soniya and Niuresha), or observing "black spots" (freckles) on women's faces during pregnancy (Rosina). Niuresha had Western biomedical knowledge of birthing that had been rote learned and but not understood. Like the pilot workshops, the women conceptualized pregnancy in clay as an outer body experience.

In the workshop at Asha Nepal, Soniya (a Brahmin,18, unmarried) created a container in clay to represent a uterus. She also made a foetus outside of it. She then led a discussion where Niuresha, Rosina, and Sulob manipulated the clay to create the different body parts associated with the process of birthing to work how it occurs (see also Ong, Mellor and Chettri 2020). It was an illumination of clay's potential in reproductive health education and an expression of inner female reproductive body knowledge.

In the workshop at CAP Nepal, Aisha (a Chettri, 20, married, with one daughter) created a clay sculpture of herself giving birth to her daughter Laxmi (see Figure 4.4).

On close inspection, the sculpture was revealing: she had clearly given birth in "stirrups". However, she did not want to talk about her clay work. We respected this. We think the 'why' became clear in the

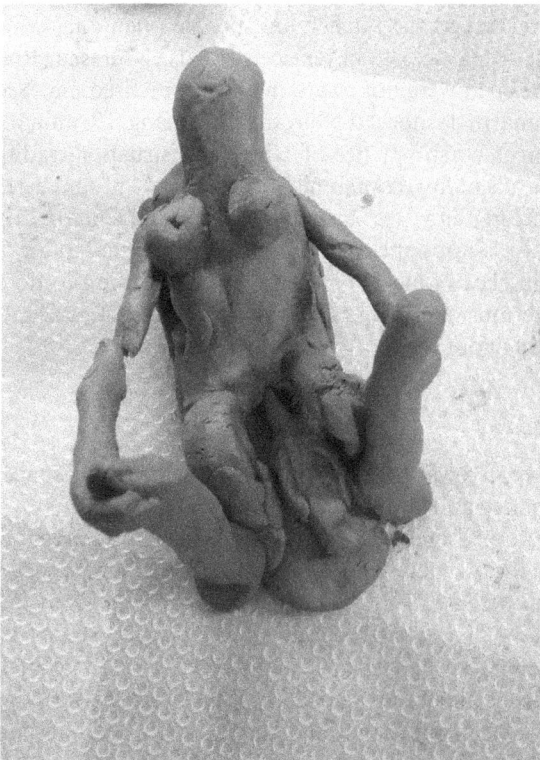

Figure 4.4 Aisha's clay sculpture of her giving birth to Laxmi in stirrups
Credit: Tricia Ong.

group interview when one of her clay work photographs triggered a memory of maternal loss.

Workshop 6: Male reproductive body

The aim of Workshop 6 for the women to produce their conceptualization of male reproductive body parts.

For this workshop, all the women created sculptures of the penis and scrotum. In both clay work and conversation, they displayed quite some knowledge of the penis. Although she moulded a penis, Soniya (a Brahmin,18, unmarried) was an exception, being very quiet in the workshop at Asha Nepal. We surmised that the topic was a particularly sensitive one for her. Just when the women were about to share their clay work, Niuresha (a Tamang, 17, unmarried) looked around and saw what the other girls had made. She then realized her penis sculpture was explicit and, clearly embarrassed, threw her body over her clay work to cover it. Sabrina and I assured her it was not something to be ashamed of having created or to share thoughts on. She then felt comfortable to show everyone. Realizing this, the women openly talked about the different terms they knew for penis from their ethnic groups (see also Ong 2018). Notably, though, for the most part, the women used the colloquial term for penis *lado* instead of its polite Nepali term (*linga*).

In the workshop at CAP Nepal, Aisha (a Chettri, 20, married, with one daughter) created a clay sculpture of a penis she said was her grandfather's, and another of her husband, naked with a penis. She told us how she first learned about a penis: "I came to know about this [pointing to the clay sculpture of her grandfather's penis] because I saw during a *saradya* [burial ritual] my grandfather was doing and he was wearing a *dhoti* [traditional dress] and that's when I saw it". The sight of her grandfather's penis had frightened her. She later used the moulded clay, and remoulded the sculpture of her grandfather's penis to demonstrate the process of erection, but the angle was incorrect. She believed that if a penis becomes erect, it goes into a rigidly 90-degree position relative to the body ("vertical" relative to the "supine" position).

Others, such as Niuresha in the Asha Nepal workshop, believed this too: "It's not upward…It would break if it is up".

Workshop 7: Outer and inner female reproductive body

The aim of Workshop 7 was to use clay work to bring up additional issues on the outer or inner female reproductive body.

In the workshop at Asha Nepal, Rosina, Niuresha, Soniya, and Sulob collectively decided to return to the topic of pregnancy. Niuresha (a Tamang, 17, unmarried) helped assign one aspect of the topic to each woman: outer body, inner body, birthing, contraception. She sculptured a detailed "vagina" and made figures of different contraceptives: "Norplant" implants, pills, and a condom. Rosina (a Magar girl, 14, unmarried) also created a "vagina". Sulob (a Tamang, 18, unmarried) made a pregnant woman. Soniya (a Brahmin,18, unmarried) created a uterus and foetus. I signalled to Sabrina to shift the focus of the discussion to Soniya's clay work because I saw an opportunity for an interesting discussion about pregnancy. The women then manipulated Soniya's clay work (with her permission) as a medium to explore the pregnancy and birthing themes from the Week 5 workshop, with some prompting from us as questions to them. This was an exciting process to watch as, through manipulating the body parts made in clay, they worked out – for themselves – how they worked. The only part they did not work out was that fluid sits around the foetus. Niuresha (a Tamang, 17, unmarried) had an "illumination": she realized that some of the biomedical knowledge she had rote-learned about the uterus at birth could be applied to model of the uterus she saw in the clay. It was magical to watch her discovery of thinking about the inner female reproductive body. In this workshop, we could also see how much reproductive body knowledge these women had accumulated from each other and through self-discovery in the seven clay body-mapping workshops (see also Ong, Mellor and Chettri 2020).

The group interview using photoethnography

The aim of the group interview component of CERM in our study was to gather more, and deeper, insights into the women's knowledge and perspectives of the female and male reproductive bodies using photographs of their clay work from the workshops taken by the women themselves or by Sabrina or me. I had these enlarged to A4 size, and Sabrina and I handed these out to their creators in individual envelopes without explanation. So, there was much excitement in the opening of envelopes and time spent looking at photographs of their work and at photographs of the others. The women had mostly forgotten about the clay work they had previously done.

We asked them to choose the photograph they most liked of their own clay work, and one they did not, and, one by one, to share their thoughts on each and on the photographs chosen by the others. Here is some of the rich discussion that followed.

The Asha Nepal group (Niuresha, Rosina, Soniya, and Sulob) all picked out, independently, photographs of their clay work from the workshop on the male reproductive body as the one they most disliked. Soniya (a Brahmin,18, unmarried) explained she had been afraid to talk about penises in the workshop:

> I don't particularly hate it [penis], but then since there are a lot of stuffs going on like 8-year-old girls getting raped in Nepali culture and also the reason is when men use women, as per their wish, and leave as per their wish so that's why I don't like it.

Over her penis photo, Rosina (a Magar girl, 14, unmarried) described an incident of domestic violence by her stepfather, who was her trafficker. Sulob (a Tamang, 18, unmarried) also related an incident of domestic violence on her mother. As that group interview progressed, the women began to talk about their mothers. Sabrina then asked them about becoming mothers and whether they had thought about their birth mothers during the clay workshops. All eyes were downcast, and all went silent. The moment was emotional, and Sabrina and I could probe no further.

Aisha (a Chettri, 20, married, with one daughter) chose the photograph of her anatomically incorrect uterus figurine from the final clay workshop on the outer and inner female reproductive body. When asked why, she related the story of her traumatic miscarriage of twin boys in a dance bar (see also Ong, Mellor and Chettri 2019). Aisha talked about people in the violent entertainment-cum-sex industry in Nepal, and that her husband had introduced her to dance bar work. He was a dancer and possibly part of the network that trafficked her.

It was her photograph of the figurines of her husband and her grandfather's penis that she most disliked. She spoke angrily of her husband's extramarital affairs, his familial neglect, and how she was thinking of returning to dance bar work because he was not supporting her or their daughter. She had not done so yet because she was concerned about being separated from her daughter during the work, and her daughter then would be exposed to women drinking. We believe she was nevertheless likely to do so because she was living in extreme impoverishment (see also Ong, Mellor and Chettri 2021).

Transcription and translation

Sabrina began transcribing the audio recordings (in Nepali) of the workshops and group interviews after the first of the clay workshops. It was a complex process because of the participatory nature and interwovenness of the discussions, and time consuming. She later translated the transcriptions into English. This entire process was additionally challenging because of electricity outages at her home, and she often stayed up until late in the night to get electricity to do the work. She became exhausted, among our other fieldwork challenges (see Chapter 6). Recognizing this, we ended up working together on the last past of the translation process over many cups of tea at a guest house close to her home. The analysis of the translated work would be carried out in Australia.

Model of the Clay Embodiment Research Method

Our configuration of CERM worked well and the experience of its development and use gives us – those who were immersed in its use

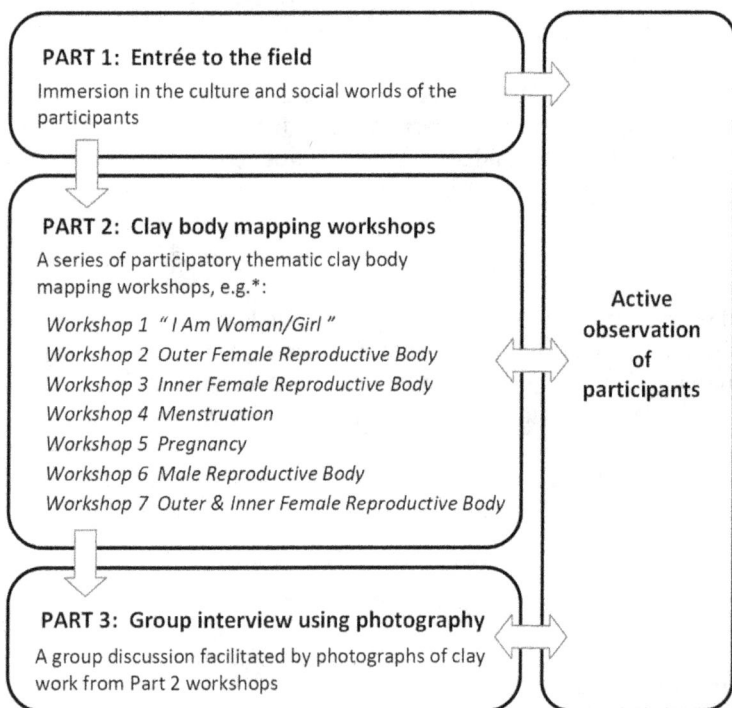

* Workshop example from Ong (2018), and Ong, Mellor and Chettri (2019, 2020, 2021).

Figure 4.5 The Clay Embodiment Research Method

and those who closely monitored our study – confidence that it can be adapted to suit other research and educational contexts. Notably, this is where words or diagrams of themselves are unlikely to help adequately convey one's internalized images that constitute personal knowledge, understanding, and beliefs. Most likely this will be with populations with low literacy or within cultures that do not rely on written communication to convey personal meaning. We may even find it useful where words, regardless of our skills with them, fail us.

Notwithstanding the irony that this book is of words and pictures, we can represent CERM as the diagram set out in Figure 4.5. The key point is that it is the interplay of four basic components – derived from theoretical frameworks and experiential insights – that produces the awareness and understanding sought in its use. These are: the phase of entrée to the field; continual active participant observation; carefully themed clay body-mapping workshops; and a group interview using photographs of clay work from the body-mapping workshops.

Conclusion

This chapter explores the development of CERM from its inspiration – how naturally sex-trafficked women in Nepal work in three dimensions with clay, and how photography was a powerful way to stimulate discussion by the women on reproductive health issues in Nepal. CERM's development is driven by lessons learnt from earlier clay body-mapping workshops, and by the advice of remarkable people in Nepal, notably Smriti Khadka, of Asha Nepal, and Nirmala Prajapati, with her deep expertise in delivering ASRH education in Nepal's schools. The lessons learned include the danger of how clay can spontaneously trigger trauma and memories because, for the Nepalese sex-trafficked women, it strongly connects to the body. This affirmed the importance of our planned thematic approach with the clay body-mapping workshops to soften trauma that might emerge.

We discuss the implementation of each of CERM's main components in our research's fieldwork. Its use with the young Nepalese sex-trafficked women with low literacy showed the power of clay and intimately connected photographs in exploring their reproductive health knowledge. The next chapter discusses the ethical considerations of designing a new research method in a complex culture highlighting Australian and Nepal perspectives and the consent process for our research participants.

References

Art2Healing. 2017. Home. https://www.arttohealing.org/ [Accessed 12 March 2022].

Asha Nepal. 2021. Home. https://asha-nepal.org/ [Accessed 12 March 2022].

Bendelow, G. 1993. Using visual imagery to explore gendered notions of pain. In: C. Renzetti and R. Lee, eds, *Researching sensitive topics*. Newbury Park: Sage, 212–28.

Crawford, M., Menger, L. and Kaufman, M.,2014. "This is a natural process": managing menstrual stigma in Nepal. *Culture, Health and* Sexuality, 16(4), 426–39.

Ong, P. 2018. *Reproductive health for the marginalised: knowledge of young women trafficked into the sex industry in Nepal*. Thesis (PhD). Deakin University.

Ong T., Mellor, D. and Chettri, S. 2019. Multiplicity of stigma: the experiences, fears and knowledge of young trafficked women in Nepal. *Sexual and Reproductive Health Matters*, 27(3), 32–48.

Ong, T., Mellor, D. and Chettri, S. 2020. Clay as a medium in three-dimensional body-mapping. *Forum: Qualitative Social Research*, 21(2), art. 9. https://www.qualitative-research.net/index.php/fqs/article/download/3380/4567?inline=1 [Accessed 12 March 2022].

Ong, T., Mellor, D. and Chettri, S. 2021. "Females are always dominated and disregarded by males, just because they are female": the continuation of patriarchal norms for young trafficked women in Nepal. *Culture, Health and Sexuality*, 1–16.

5 The ethical considerations of designing a new research method in a complex culture

Australian and Nepal perspectives

Introduction

As an Australian researcher planning to undertake a "culturally sensitive" research using a new methodology involving young women who had been trafficked into the sex industry in Nepal with low literacy, one of the more interesting challenges I faced was formulating the ethical approach for it. This had to satisfy my educational institution (Deakin University, Australia) and the Nepal Health Research Council. While the exploration of the ethics of the research itself was deeply complex and fascinating, what made it more so was the difference in perspectives of the two ethics approval bodies.

This chapter discusses both the processes of seeking ethics approval for this "high risk" research project and the ethics issues that give rise to the high level of risk involved. Its intention is to illuminate ethics issues with the use of CERM in the conditions it was designed for (i.e., sex-trafficked women in Nepal with low literacy) by using our experience as a guide.

Ethics approval in Australia

To begin with, our research project required the approval of Deakin University, Australia, specifically its School of Health and Social Development, and, separately, Deakin University Human Research Ethics Committee (DUHREC). The process leading up to the final approval of the research is one clearly mapped out as a series of steps and decisions: completing an ethics programme, research project development and approval, an application expressly for ethics approval of high-risk research, and preliminary and full review of the application.

DOI: 10.4324/b23275-5

Ethics training and approval of research scope, methodology, and management

All aspiring researchers at Deakin University must have passed an ethics programme before having any involvement with research involving human participants. Developed and delivered online by the university's Human Research Ethics Office, the programme covers the fundamental concerns of ethics in research – including issues of consent, dealing with minors, and risk assessment – and is intended to be relevant regardless of the level of ethical risk that the research may entail.

Moreover, research proposals at the University are, of course, subject to various reviews and approvals. In the case of my study using CERM, its review was by a panel constituted by the University as the key part of a process for confirmation of candidature for Doctor of Philosophy. It comprised experts in my field of research and the higher degrees by the research coordinator for the School of Health and Social Development, this being my School at the time. The panel's primary concerns were that the study is feasible, worthwhile, well planned and could be well executed. It needed to understand the study's aims and methodology, resourcing, and timelines, and the degree of knowledge, expertise, and motivation that would drive the multi-year study through variable circumstances.

In preparing my proposal to the panel, I had generous guidance and challenge from my primary supervisor, Professor David Mellor, and associate supervisor, Dr. Maria Pallotti-Chiarolli. They were there to support my presentation to the panel, as was, at my request, Dr. Sabitra Kaphle, a female Nepali who undertook doctoral research on maternal health in the remote rural district of Mugu in Nepal. So, at my presentation to the panel, I had a person present who knew the cultural and reproductive health context of my study. Referencing her observations in the field, I discussed the inspiration for CERM as born of the necessity to engage with Nepalese women with low literacy more meaningfully.

To demonstrate to the panel the use of the clay body-mapping component of CERM with the women in Nepal, I created a circle on the floor of the presentation room using six pieces of paper – one for myself, my potential research assistant, and four research participants – and put a hand-sized ball of clay on each. I explained how I would enable the women to work with the clay, how we would use my flexible questionnaire, and how I (or the women and girls) would then photograph the clay work at the end of each planned workshop to use in a group interview later. This small demonstration helped the panel to conceptualize

CERM, and I think it also reinforced the importance of the cultural context for women in Nepal (e.g., clay is a familiar medium to them and they often sit in circles) and the relevance of my art therapy background and experience with the use of clay with women in Nepal. Dr. Kaphle added context and offered her perspective during the demonstration. The panel approved my project.

Ethics-specific approval

As is common Australian university practice, my research proposal was further assessed for its ethical implications. At Deakin University, its Human Research Ethics Office assesses the degree of care a research project is likely to require for ethics integrity. The objective is, of course, the thoughtful protection of the research participants, researchers, relevant third parties, and the University itself, from harm caused by the proposed research. As one where important ethical consideration arise, my research proposal was assessed as requiring specific approval of the DUHREC ("the Ethics Committee") notwithstanding its earlier approval by the confirmation of candidature panel.

For the Ethics Committee to grant its approval, it had to be satisfied that the research meets the expectations set out by Australia's National Health and Medical Research Council's *National Statement on Ethical Conduct in Human Research* and its *Australian Code for the Responsible Conduct of Research* (as they applied at the time). Guided by a helpful application process, the information I provided to the Ethics Committee focussed on the research participants to be recruited, how they were to be recruited, and the nature of their participation. It included a comprehensive risk management plan – the highest evaluated risk being the emergence of reproductive health trauma for both research participants and researchers – and the mechanism for consent to be used by young Nepali women with low literacy. The consent we settled on (discussed later in this chapter) had considerable input from Dr. Kaphle, my supervisors, and advisors from the Human Research Ethics Office, and was translated into Nepali by Dr. Kaphle.

The Ethics Committee considered the 60-plus page application and approved the research study. The next step was to seek its approval in Nepal.

Ethics approval in Nepal

All health-related research in Nepal is required to have approval to do so from the NHRC, a statutory body charged with promoting and coordinating health research in that country with the objective of improving the health status of people of Nepal (see Nepal Health Research Council 2020). As is clear from its application form, the NHRC's consideration focusses on the ethics of the proposed research – the review and approval of applications is by its Ethical Review Board, assisted by Institutional Review Committees based within health institutions acting with the Board's delegated authority. Actual compliance by researchers with the requirement to have NHRC approval to conduct their research may be questionable (Sharma, Khatri and Harper 2016). Yet the benefits for researchers in applying for approval goes beyond merely keeping within the law of the land. For our research, for example, it provided an opportunity for thoughtful feedback and validation of the appropriateness of our approach and methods in the context of Nepalese culture. The application also gave the proposed study visibility to people (NHRC members and appointees) who are well connected within the local political, heath, and research establishment as well as aid agencies working in the country.

The devastating 25 April 2015 earthquake near Kathmandu and the thousands of aftershocks halted the work needed to be done in Nepal to proceed with our research study. Indeed, for some months I was not sure if our study would go ahead at all – there was the physical risk, and my funding would be cancelled on 30 November if the study's field-work in Nepal had not begun. Most distressing of all was the impact of the earthquake on my primary partner organization for the study, Asha Nepal based in Kathmandu where the study was to be based. Smriti Khadka, the manager of Asha Nepal and a key support for the study, not only faced a difficult task in recovering that organization's services, but also worked with other anti-trafficking organizations in Nepal to push the Government of Nepal to stop the movement of orphaned children from their districts of origins to others for fear of trafficking.

By July 2015, though, the situation in Kathmandu had improved sufficiently that we could continue our planning, including submitting our application to the NHRC. In this we received advice and much help from our Nepal partners on what matters for Nepalese decision makers, and this underlies the tremendous advantage of having established connections locally who can provide cultural orientation.

In comparison to the Australian review process, the Nepal one seemed much less comprehensive. On first review on email, the NHRC Ethical Review Board only had a few questions about the project. However, after a circuitous email process of questions about my research methods, the Board suggested I make a ten-minute presentation at one of its meetings (see Figure 5.1). This occurred on 4 November, and I had with me

Figure 5.1 Nepal Health Research Council, Kathmandu, Nepal

Nirmala Prajapati, who was one of my early co-investigators. She had held several health-related roles in Nepal, so understood the review process. She had also helped me in the early stage of my research planning (see Chapter 4). At the presentation she, through visual cues, guided me on how the Board was receiving my presentation and answers to their questions, which was generally positively.

Of particular interest to the Board was the validity of CERM given it was new. However, once I explained it in the context of ethnography and PAR, the Board members seemed to appreciate it, perhaps because ethnography and PAR are relatively well known in Nepal. The other main line of questioning sought assurance on working with Nepalese research assistants. Towards the end of the meeting, a male member of the Board cautioned me about the "culturally sensitive" nature of the study – in relation to both sex trafficking and reproductive health contexts – not as a deterrent to undertaking it but to ensure I adopted a sensitive approach.

It was especially surprising to me that the Board did not ask detailed questions about the study's scope or information about young girls (under 18 years) who have been sex trafficked. I think this is because the Nepalese cultural view of female aging emphasizes biological markers – puberty and menstruation being the key ones for the young – rather than chronological progression. Hence, it seems normal in Nepal to see young girls take on care-giving roles or be the subject of marriage considerations, more so in rural regions (which is where most of Nepal's population reside).

Afterwards the Board emailed me a few follow-up questions about my methods. It granted its approval 12 days after my presentation, and my fieldwork began two weeks after that, on the last day that I had to have begun it to maintain my funding.

Young Nepalese sex-trafficked women and girls with low literacy and consent

The research plan called for recruiting young women aged 13 to 18 years who had entered the reproductive life stage (i.e., begun menstruating) with scope to increase the upper range to 22 years if, as was the case as it turned out, there were greater than anticipated difficulties in accessing young sex-trafficked women at our main partner organization, Asha Nepal. The plan limited the number of women recruited to not more than ten, in consideration of the sensitivity of the study's subject, the anticipated young age of participants and their vulnerability to reproductive trauma, and their expected low levels of literacy. In Nepal, although there is no stereotypical trafficked girl (Crawford 2017), many are "relatively poor, young, unmarried, and less educated migrant girls and women from the rural hills and mountain regions of Nepal" (Hamal Gurung (2014: 169).

One of the big ethical challenges then was to be confident that the women and children in our study fully and properly consented to participating in it. With the children, article 12 of the United Nation's Convention on the Rights of the Child "assures, to every child capable of forming his or her own views, the right to express those views freely in all matters affecting the child, the views of the child being given due weight in accordance with age and maturity" (Office of the United Nations High Commissioner for Human Rights 2022). It is especially important in our case as parents and family members may have facilitated the sex trafficking of the child and, if so, are wholly unreliable as a guardian for matters of consent. However, we also gained guardianship and organizational consent from Asha Nepal and CAP Nepal, our research partners, because the women and girls were beneficiaries of their care.

For their menstruation research with women in Nepal, Crawford, Menger and Kaufman (2014) used audio recording for verbal consent. This, too, was our initial plan, but when in Nepal I felt audio recording with verbal explanation and verbal consent was not enough for our young low literate research participants. So, I added visual forms to the consent process. Along with a very simple "Plain Language Statement for Verbal Consent" (translated into Nepali), I created a series of A4-sized posters with outlines of a body drawn on computer by my Nepalese friend Avinash Shrestha to help explain the study and its components, in particular the clay body-mapping workshops. I would also use a small fabric (calico) doll I brought from Australia (as part of a gift kit for the women) to explain the themes of each of the workshops, and the focus of the subsequent group interview using photoethnography (see Figure 5.2). The idea for this came from a "wish doll kit" for creating affirmations from Krupa Devi, an art therapist who works in India (see Sankalpa Journeys 2021). I also developed another set of posters to explain the process of audio recording the workshops and group interview, photographing the women's clay work, and publishing my research findings in my thesis and journal articles. Finally, we would use an audio

Figure 5.2 Visual consent posters and a fabric doll used to gain consent from Aisha, Indira, Niuresha, Rosina, Soniya, and Sulob to gain their permission to participate our research

Credit: Tricia Ong.

recorder to record verbal consent. These changes were approved by Deakin University.

The NHRC required that we took thumbprints of the women and girls as evidence they had consented to participate in the study. However, these were not required to be provided to the NHRC and they remain on (our) file.

Post-fieldwork ethics review in Australia

Upon invitation, some months after my return from Nepal, I gave a presentation to the Ethics Committee at one of its meetings on the work done in Nepal. I shared stories from the field, photographs of the women's clay body-mapping work from CERM, the process of verbal and visual consent and more. I also described an issue related to the photographs that I had not considered before leaving Australia.

For the group interview using photoethnography component of CERM, I needed to print photographs of the women's clay work in A4 size. I had befriended a woman who ran a stationery and printing shop in Lazimpat, one of two foreign embassy districts in Kathmandu. On the day I went to have the photographs of the clay work photos of the male reproductive body (i.e., penises) printed – I had to print photographs in stages due to electricity outages in the city – the small shop was full of people. I became aware that people could see these revealing photographs on the printer. Fortunately, the electricity stopped – along with the printer – which gave me an opportunity to explain the sensitivity of the photographs to the shop's owner. After this, she printed them for me when no one was around and put them in an A4 size envelope I had bought from her.

We had a good discussion at the Ethics Committee meeting about what the incident and the cultural context in which it occurred could teach us about exploring ethical issues, notably that for novel projects or ones in unusual settings it is useful to work out even innocuous steps and events when identifying potential ethical problems. There was also a good discussion about my adapting the consent process once the limitations of its original design became clear on the ground, and how this can be built in as a review step in other research the Committee would consider. Afterwards, one of the human research ethics advisors present at the meeting asked to use our application for ethics approval as an "exemplar" of a "high-risk" study application that other researchers could consider in formulating their own application. The discussion also led to an invitation to share our learnings from the field as a panellist at Victorian Ethics Network "Recherche sans Frontiere Hypothetical session", as part of an ethics conference in Melbourne, Australia.

Conclusion

A key point to make is that our research study was enhanced for having gone through the thinking, application, questioning, and feedback of ethics approval processes both in Australia and Nepal. When examining the application forms one fills in to gain ethics approval for human research, we see considerable overlap of information sought by the Australian-based approving body and that by the Nepal-based one. This is hardly surprising – the core principles and considerations of ethical human research are well established, so research institutions globally are likely to have a similar checklist of assurances when considering research proposals. However, I have realized from my experience of the ethics approval process in Nepal that there can be significant (to the point of being surprising) local differences of emphasis that are rooted in cultural norms. The other lesson for me in seeking approval is how valuable it was to have a knowledgeable local person to work with us to appreciate the subtleties of concerns raised by local ethics assessors. The value is not merely gaining the approval, but also a clearer understanding of the social environment in which the research is to take place, and so improving the quality of its planning.

References

Crawford, M. 2017. International sex trafficking. *Women and Therapy*, 40(1–2), 101–22.

Crawford, M., Menger, L. and, Kaufman, M. 2014. "This is a natural process"': managing menstrual stigma in Nepal. *Culture, Health and Sexuality*, 16(4), 426–39.

Hamal Gurung, S. 2014. Sex trafficking and the sex trade industry: the processes and experiences of Nepali Women. *Journal of Intercultural Studies*, 35(2), 163–81.

Nepal Health Research Council. 2020. *About*. Kathmandu: Nepal Health Research Council. http://nhrc.gov.np/about/. [Accessed 5 April 2022].

Office of the United Nations High Commissioner for Human Rights. 2022.*Convention on the Rights of the Child*. Geneva: Office of the United Nations High Commissioner for Human Rights. https://www.ohchr.org/en/instruments-mechanisms/instruments/convention-rights-child [Accessed 7 April 2022].

Sankalpa Art Journeys. 2021. *Products*. Auroville: Sankalpa. https://www.sanka lpajourneys.com/products [Accessed 7 April 2022].

Sharma, R.J., Khatri, R. and Harper, I. 2016. Understanding Health Research Ethics in Nepal. *Developing World Bioethics,* 16(3), 140–7. https://onlinelibr ary.wiley.com/doi/10.1111/dewb.12109 [Accessed 7 April 2022].

6 The (im)practicalities of using clay in Nepal

Mayhem and messiness

Introduction

CERM is underpinned foundationally by clay. While at first glance clay was a culturally appropriate material for our research participants, we faced challenges to using it at time we carried out fieldwork in Nepal (November 2015–April 2016) in large part due to unexpected environmental conditions – the aftermath of two major earthquakes, a border blockade with India (September 2015–February 2016), and increased pollution resulting from both – and the variable quality of Nepali clay. This chapter explores these (im)practicalities of using clay and how it prompted us to adapt our approaches for all challenges.

Transportation

My first practical task in setting up the fieldwork for my research in Nepal was to source local materials, particularly clay. Local materials can help to reduce resistance to engaging in research for illiterate populations in Nepal (Butcher and Kievelitz 1997). Getting the materials was unusually difficult, as seven months earlier Nepal had its worst earthquake in 80 years. This severely disrupted the lives of people across the country and services, including the operations of my local partner organization, Asha Nepal. Then, just before starting my fieldwork, a minority ethnic group residing on the border with India – the Madhesi – blocked passage across the border in protest against a proposed new Nepalese constitution (see Tripathi 2019). Since India is a major source of goods for Nepal, the blockage created shortages of food, fuel, gas, medicine, and other necessities. This, in turn, severely affected the availability and cost of transportation, one result of which was that clay supplies had dried up in Kathmandu. I had to figure out how to source clay from Thimi, a town nine kilometres outside the

DOI: 10.4324/b23275-6

Kathmandu Valley, where a lot of pottery is made without it costing much more than my meagre fieldwork budget had allowed.

I asked my local contacts for suggestions and an artist friend of mine, Sarita Dongol, who runs clay workshops at Community Children's Art School (CCAS), came to my rescue. She got a friend of hers to pick her up by motorcycle, travel to Thimi to buy clay, and to then meet me in the old city of Pātan. I paid her for the clay (approx. $10AUS for ten kilograms) and gave the motorbike rider a generous tip for his help. Still fearing I might not have enough clay, and only being in Nepal for a brief visit to assess the earthquake damage and impact on my project, on my return to Australia I purchased ten additional kilograms of clay to bring back to Nepal. My research supervisor was concerned the clay would not be allowed through Nepali customs, but it landed safely along with the rest of my research toolkit (audio recorder, camera, plastic mats for floors, notebook, tablet, etc.). Fortunately, everything else I needed – including *diyos* (small clay oil lamps used in religious rituals) – was available at local markets and shops in Kathmandu.

The fuel shortage also made travel to field sites more difficult for me, my research assistant, and the research participants. Based on prior experience of conditions in Kathmandu, and given the heaviness of the clay and not being able to store it at field sites, I had planned to use taxis. Now there were hardly any on the roads. Many were sitting in kilometres-long queues for petrol for days, their drivers sleeping in their cars, so they did not lose their place. The few on the road charged significantly more – and even more for obvious foreigners – which took the regular use of taxis to be beyond the capacity of my limited fieldwork budget. So, I opted for public buses instead – they were big and cheap. It would also give me an opportunity to practise my Nepali with local people. However, the fuel shortages led to overcrowding on buses and disrupted their schedules. The clay and other research tools I carried onto buses were heavy, though I had lessened the load I planned to carry from just under ten kilograms to four to five by only carrying the exact number of hand-sized clay balls we needed for our clay workshops on the day.

Nevertheless, I was constantly worried I would injure someone on the bus with my loaded backpack, especially as the roads, which were already bumpy in Kathmandu generally, had been broken up by the earthquakes. The clay was also the source of an embarrassing incident on a micro bus. After one of our clay workshops, we had packed up in a hurry and I had clearly not sealed the plastic container containing the clay. Murky clay residue seeped onto my trousers and bus seat to the discomfort of others around me. Overcrowding and risk of injury aside, it soon dawned on me that Nepal's public buses are notorious places of sexual assault, a recent one on a female foreigner volunteer coming to mind. So, I decided that I would only travel on public buses, micro buses, *tempos* (small electric cars), when I was with Sabrina Chettri, my Nepalese research assistant and, only when absolutely necessary, taxis. I would walk the rest of the time. Largely, I got accustomed to walking with my clay backpack and enjoyed changing my route to get to know the unnamed streets, alleyways, and local people. The staff at my destination, Asha Nepal, felt encouraged to walk more after noticing me getting fitter and losing my "chubby cheeks". They often laughed at an (inaccurate) Nepali phrase I coined to express this: "*Mero pukka pukka ghala harayo*" (my fluffy/chubby cheeks got lost).

The disruption to transport also caused delays for my research assistant getting to the clay workshops on time. As I was aware that Nepalese work on a different concept of time, I had always allowed for this. However, my research assistant was often "more than late", which used to cause me frustration until I was invited to her family home. Then I realized that she was coming from across the other side of the city of Kathmandu and had to use several connecting forms of public transport to reach me. Two of our research participants were also affected by transport delays. The delays to these workshops were usually extended by also having to spend time settling their infant children after the long bus trips. It all gave me a much better understanding of the pace of "Nepali time".

Earthquakes and pollution

There were unusual environmental problems in Nepal at the time of my fieldwork that affected our health. When I arrived in Kathmandu to begin my fieldwork, the city was still experiencing aftershocks from the massive 2015 earthquake. (There were three sizable earthquakes during my stay.) While some cleaning up of debris had occurred, the city was full of collapsed buildings, broken roads, and piles of rubble. The city was unusually dusty, dirty, and chaotic. Pollution increased because of this and the consequences of the border blockade. Kathmandu already had a significant air pollution problem prior to this: it sits in the top ten countries in the world for the worst air pollution. Contributory issues are a winter inversion, which traps a dense layer of cold air, and with it high levels of pollutants, near the Kathmandu Valley. Other sources of pollution include vehicular emissions, wildfires, and cross-border industrial pollution. While transport fumes decreased during the blockade, the burning of wood fuels increased when shortages of cooking gas doubled its price – and made overt the "black market". I saw people queuing for kilometres to get gas supplies that were trickling into Nepal. At Asha Nepal and CAP Nepal the women made *chulos* (clay stoves) on the balconies and rooftops to cook for the women and girls in their care. The health consequences for women were significant: they were cooking outdoors in the depths of winter and breathing in wood fire smoke in the process.

The air pollution was as if Kathmandu was perpetually in a fog. Moving about in the city left our faces and clothes with dust and grime. I found small stones in my hair when showering. My hair fell out in clumps. Despite wearing a charcoal-filtered pollution mask while walking to field sites, my research assistant and I got sick. I contracted a chest infection that nearly sent me home to Australia in skeletal form.

The use of clay

Many types of clay are produced in Nepal and used for different purposes. The clay I needed was refined pottery clay – with low levels of impurities – and specifically the type produced in Thimi and used by potters there to make bowls, cups, curd containers, etc. Nepali clay is not as soft and pliable as Australian clay. In hot environments, it dries out quickly and becomes difficult to manipulate. In dry cold conditions it could do the same. Adding water to the dry clay could make it too soft. It is also especially messy to use. When training my research assistant on CERM we worked on Nepali clay on a sunny rooftop of our favourite tea shop, Tings Teahouse in the foreign embassy district of Lazimpat, it dried out quickly, crumbling into a powdery residue and easily scattering everywhere. Clay dust poses a health risk as the naturally occurring silica particles in it can cause permanent lung damage if breathed in. Still, sweeping up clay dust was easier than cleaning up moist clay.

On a bitterly cold winter's day after running the pilot workshops at the Mahendra Vidhya Ashram school in Barahisthan, we cleaned up the clay residue using a cold water tap outdoors. The water on our hands turned to ice and the clay became hard. As with using it anywhere else, we had to prevent is being washed down the drains lest it block the (already fragile) plumbing system. Cleaning was a stop–start process that consumed considerable time. That day, my research assistant and I decided to do a "rough clean" at the school and pack all the clay materials in my backpack to transport it back to Kathmandu the next day, where I planned to clean everything properly in my apartment with (albeit-spasmodic) hot water. However, the next morning my backpack was leaking watery clay residue. I wrapped it up as best I could, but by the time I returned to my apartment it was a big soggy mess and it took a lot of time to clean up.

Trying to find the right degree of clay malleability was sometimes frustrating for the research participants in our workshops. We captured some humorous dialogues about the "frustrations" of working with clay in our audio recordings. One of the women, Sulob, simply said: "*Katro thulo bachha bhanako. Mato nai gilo bhayecha k*" (The clay is really soft … It's not working!). Yet the women were soon getting the clay to just how they wanted it. At the pilot workshop, the women learned to use the *diyos* to add water to improve its pliability. Likewise, the research participants of the main study learned to manage the clay by using water from the *diyos* to moisten it and rolling the water out of it on the plastic mats if the clay became too soft. At the end of each workshop, the clay would often be dry from use. My research assistant and I became adept at preparing the clay for the next session. We would put a "thumb hole"

Figure 6.1 The staff counsellor at Asha Nepal holds some of the clay we gave her after the clay body-mapping workshops were completed

in the top of each ball of clay and add water. This would be absorbed, and the clay would once again become pliable and ready for the next workshop. We had no issues using the clay in the room we used at CAP Nepal. This is because it was dark and cool, which suggested it was the perfect temperature for doing clay work in Nepal.

Given the difficulties with using Nepali clay, I became "precious" about caring for it, tending to it like gardener watering plants. What I saw occur with the clay in the hands of the sex-trafficked women made the clay like gold. When we had finished using the clay in Nepal, I gave it – my Australian clay and Nepali clay – to the staff counsellor at Asha Nepal who had been taken aback by the power of clay to elicit stories of sexually abused girls in a workshop we ran together (see Chapter 4) (see Figure 6.1).

Conclusion

This chapter discusses what might have initially been perceived as the (im)practicalities of using clay in Nepal. There were issues arising from the unusual circumstances of earthquakes and the border blockade, leading to the lack of clay supplies, the disruption to public transport, the physical difficulties of carrying the clay, and exposure to dangerous levels of pollution. Then there are the issues with using Nepali clay – its quality, reactivity to hot or cold weather conditions, and messiness in use. Despite all the (im)practicalities of using clay in Nepal, we – researchers, research participants and local friends – found practical solutions to these issues. We persisted with using clay because it was evident that using it was an intuitive and highly effective means for young sex-trafficked women in Nepal with low literacy to share their reproductive health knowledge. The process was also fun, dynamic, and a fast and efficient method of collecting data collection, despite some risks in its use that will be explored in the next chapter.

References

Butcher, K. and Kievelitz, U. 1997. Planning with PRA: HIV and STD in a Nepalese mountain community. *Health and Policy Planning*, 12(3), 253–61. www.academic.oup.com/heapol/article/12/3/253/740072/ [Accessed 22 December 2021].

Tripathi, D. 2019. Influence of borders on bilateral ties in south Asia: a study of contemporary India–Nepal relations. *International Studies*, 56(2–3), 186–200.

7 The power of the Clay Embodiment Research Method

Fun, fast, and dangerous

Introduction

CERM was first designed to explore the reproductive health knowledge of young women who had been trafficked into the sex industry in Nepal. However, it is clear to us that the scope of its use has potential with other populations and in other contexts. This chapter discusses the value of CERM for body-related research with populations with low literacy and its potential for use in education. It highlights the rapidity of the method, its dangers for use and how these can be lessened by having the support of local organizations and individuals with particular expertise.

The Clay Embodiment Research Method in body-related research for populations with low literacy

One of the biggest satisfactions we got from using CERM in our research with sex-trafficked women in Nepal was seeing its value with this low literacy group. Clay, the key material of the method, is regarded as good for body-related work (Sherwood 2004, Elbrecht 2012). Our research goes further, clearly demonstrating a "match" between a dependence on learning by seeing in three dimensions, and CERM's three-dimensional (clay) body-mapping (see Ong 2018, Ong, Mellor and Chettri 2020). The fact that clay was a culturally familiar material enhanced the experience of its use by our research participants. CERM's photography component added an intimate and personal layer to the women's subsequent reflection on their experience of moulding their three-dimensional bodies in clay.

Our experience with CERM leads us to believe that it is an effective tool with populations with low literacy in cultures where traditional body-mapping techniques, such as MacCormack's (1985) technique – drawing

DOI: 10.4324/b23275-7

an outline of paper and getting research participants to fill in body parts – have not been particularly successful (see Chapter 3). One example that comes to mind of where CERM may be particularly effective is from Bennett's (2017: 115) description of body-mapping with a *belian* (traditional Indonesian midwife) in exploring infertility issues in Indonesia: "body-mapping only made sense for *belian* when it was literally performed on and through the body".

The Clay Embodiment Research Method in education

It was also clear that, in the course of our clay body-mapping workshops and group interview using photography, the women in our study realized mistaken assumptions they had about reproductive health and took delight in discovering new knowledge. (see Ong, Mellor and Chettri 2020). These were essentially self-discoveries shared among the group rather than explanations from either my research assistant or me, tempted as we were, as education was outside the scope of our study. We know some of the women left the workshops with inaccurate knowledge from either copying the work of their peers or because parts of the body were invisible (see Ong, Mellor and Chettri 2020). Nevertheless, their experience was one of eliciting and sharing perceptions, assumptions, and knowledge through the medium of clay. If, when looking at the work of their peers, they observed a body part missing in their own clay figures, they would mould it and add it to their sculpture. This process was fun as the women challenged each other's representations – it facilitated rich in-depth discussion about reproductive health. The focus and value placed on their expressions of their "experiential knowledge" of their bodies seemed empowering for them, an act of self-dignity. My research assistant also learned about reproductive health issues in this process, especially from the married women who had given birth. This experience was empowering for these women (see Ong 2018). We could see in all these the power of clay use in an educational context for similarly low-literate population groups.

A time-responsive method

A key constraint the study faced was time spent on fieldwork in Nepal: the timing of its start and its duration. This was, in effect, imposed by the terms of my research funding and made even more challenging by delays caused by the massive 2015 earthquake and 2015–16 economic blockade at the Nepal–India border. The fact that we were able to complete the fieldwork and extract good quality research data from it in the time available owes much to intense planning beforehand and the help and cooperation of the organizations and people on the ground in Nepal.

Moreover, it was CERM itself that provided a streamlined sequence of activities, producing data in the significantly shorter time than using a comparable sequence of conventional methods such as (traditional) ethnography or PAR. Of course, time taken with the conventional methods will depend on the purpose and context to which they are applied. For those familiar with these, it may be useful to note that our CERM clay workshops lasted between 45 and 60 minutes each, depending on the level of energy of the women on the day and the intensity and richness of discussion. The other constraint on time was our – my research assistant and I – own energy levels. In addition to facilitating them, throughout each workshop and group discussions we needed to keep eye contact with one another as a means of subtle communication, observe the women's body language, listen to their voices, and to watch for the elicitation of trauma and spontaneous emergences of distress while engaging in clay.

Surprisingly, we did not use the CERM flexible interview questionnaires as much as planned because the participatory discussion facilitated by the clay body-mapping was rich of its own accord. Only on occasion did I need to prompt my research assistant to ask for additional detail on issues from the women. Only after my research assistant transcribed the audio recordings into Nepali and translated them into English, and we looked at the photographs of the clay work alongside, did we realize just how much information we had collected in each short workshop. It was complex to analyze because of the participatory discussions, but provided a rich basis for my thesis and subsequent journal papers on that work.

Dangers in the use of the Clay Embodiment Research Method

Although we see CERM as ideal for use with low-literate populations and where cultural sensitivities are critical, we also foresee dangers in its use with some population groups. In the case of our study, my primary concern was the spontaneous elicitation of trauma in the clay workshops. I was also on the lookout for stress responses during discussions of sex, this being a taboo subject for Nepalese women (Harman, Kaufman and Shrestha 2014). Sometimes the women refused to talk about reproductive body parts they made with clay, or expressed embarrassment, or simply did not make explicit ones (i.e., "vagina" (vulva) and penis), (see Chapter 4). We learned how important it is to

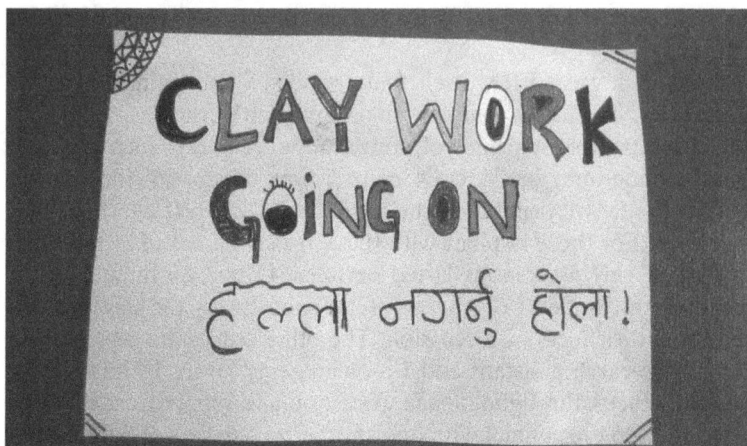

Figure 7.1 "Clay work going on"

have a cloth in our clay kit that the women could use to cover their clay creations. However, we were mostly able to get the women to talk about their clay works by assuring them it was a safe space to do so. Some of the non-research participants at Asha Nepal made a poster to stop people entering the room when clay workshops were being run there (see Figure 7.1) after an unintentional intrusion by a staff member at CAP Nepal, which caused embarrassment for one of our research participants (see Chapter 4). Developing trusting relationships prior to beginning CERM proved important to encouraging the women to participate in its processes.

The prospect of trauma or unintended catharsis reinforces the point about the intimate connection between the women's clay body-mapping and photography of it, with their feelings about their reproductive body. It also reinforces the need for training in CERM – body-mapping, the therapeutic use of clay, and associated use of photography. Recent work on body-mapping alone has reinforced the need for training for its use in research, education or therapy (Jager et al. 2016, Orchard 2017, Boydell et al. 2020, Ong, Mellor and Chettri 2020, Solomon 2020), with proper psychological support (Solomon 2020). Body-mapping, if conducted in an unsafe environment and/or with untrained facilitators, can lead to retraumatizing participants (Solomon 2020).

There were, for the women, instances when, on reflecting on the photographs of their clay work, stories of trauma emerged. For example, photographs of "penises" in clay evoked images of sexual violence by men and talk about the gang rape of 8–9-year-old Nepali girls. A photograph of an "anatomically incorrect" uterus triggered a woman's memory of miscarriage of twin boys in a dance bar due to a violent incident. A woman who had remained silent when it came to discussing her clay work of giving birth in the pregnancy-themed workshop revealed her miscarriage in the group interview with photography, and later thanked us for the opportunity to share her pregnancy experiences. My research assistant and I suspect that she had never shared her experience before. The use of photographs in the context of an interview has been known to be quite personal for participants and researchers (see Chapter 4). However, in the interview where the miscarriage was revealed, I paused the interview because my research assistant also became emotional. Later, in our debriefing sessions, she said it had really upset her. I offered her external counselling, but she ended up talking about her experience with perhaps the best person for her: her mother.

Drawing on expertise

A creative arts therapist as researcher

Creating clay body sculptures can elicit trauma. We saw this in workshops with sexually abused girls and the sex-trafficked women. Reflecting on photographs of the reproductive bodies and then discussing them can also do the same. The spontaneous emergences of strong emotions in some of our workshops and in the group discussion was not a surprise. Clay therapists speak of its therapeutic power (Sherwood 2004, Elbrecht 2012). To that end, Liamputtong (2007) points out that sensitive research with vulnerable populations needs to be undertaken with researchers who have therapeutic training to make a psychologically space safe for the research participants. I agree with both views and add that good knowledge of the cultural context in which the research is conducted is also critical for the safe use of clay with vulnerable women in Nepal.

My own training and experience as a creative arts therapist specializing in women's reproductive health not only provided a foundational approach to CERM, but it also gave me confidence in monitoring the spontaneous emergences from clay of the women in the workshops and group discussion. Moreover, I had previously worked with Asha Nepal, the study's partner organization in Nepal, in running a reproductive health workshop for adolescent girls and, separately, with sexually abused girls. I believe our close collaboration on these especially provided Asha Nepal's manager, Smriti Khadka, gave confidence that the women in our study – to whom she facilitated us access – would be in a safe environment throughout their participation.

A young female bilingual Nepali research asistant

It is evident to me that, of the many factors that contributed to CERM working well in our study, a critical one was having Sabrina Chettri as my Nepalese research assistant during the fieldwork. Her remarkable work as research assistant, interpreter, and translator aside, CERM worked well for us in no small measure because the women of our study found her to be highly relatable notwithstanding that (or perhaps in part because) she did not have any experience of their particular trauma and hardships. Here is a short story of how I found her, which may throw light on the importance of a connecting bridge between researcher and research participants in CERM projects.

In Nepal, researchers have used Nepalese university graduates experienced in conducting research on sensitive topics as research assistants, although generally only female research assistants are involved in the data collection (contact with the research participants) because of the sensitivity (see Puri, Shah and Tamang 2010, Lamichhane et al. 2011, Puri, Tamang and Shah 2011, Puri et al. 2012). Others have also noted that it is not possible to conduct interviews on sexual issues with the opposite sex in Nepal (Regmi et al. 2011).

The previously mentioned Smriti Khadka suggested that I look for a young Nepalese university graduate with no exposure to research in sex-trafficking rather than someone with strong experience in it who may then sway our research to their own strongly held views. So it was that one of the social workers at Asha Nepal, Uzen Malla, reached out to a young female bilingual Nepali social work graduate, Sabrina Chettri, who had helped facilitate ASRH workshops run by the Family Planning Association of Nepal (FPAN). Smriti, Uzen, and I jointly interviewed her. She was energetic, youthful, and funny. I immediately warmed to her. She also showed a genuine interest in art therapy. After the interview, Smriti looked at me and said the word "*Ananda*" (bliss) – we had found the right person. However, Smriti also cautioned me to ensure Sabrina understood the difference between "research" and "education" because of her background with FPAN to ensure she did not step into an educator role.

Sabrina accompanied me on visits to the field sites of our partner organizations, Asha Nepal and CAP Nepal, to get to know our potential research participants. We spent time together clay-making as training in the use of CERM, including how we would set up the workshops, what we would if trauma was elicited, and how we would debrief. I discovered she had a penchant for origami and used that skill to make beautiful clay sculptures. The training was also a trust-building exercise for both of us. We found it easy to discuss issues, whether research related or personal. As our get-togethers involved lots of tea drinking and eating cake, we had lots of fun.

Yet, choosing a local as the research assistant and interpreter produced an immediate problem. While we started well with getting to know some of the potential research participants from Asha Nepal, others told Smriti that they did not trust Sabrina to keep their confidences because of a perceived "gossip culture" among Nepalese women. Somehow, Smriti won them over, perhaps because they trusted her and she said she trusted us. Smriti also pointed out to the girls that Sabrina had signed a confidentiality agreement with Asha Nepal and independently with me. She explained how reliant I was on Sabrina for my research because I could only speak and understand basic Nepali. When Smriti told us of their initial apprehension, Sabrina and I developed a strategy – whenever we visited the girls, we would always arrive together to show the women we were a team. This seemed to have worked judging by the enthusiasm the unmarried trafficked women later showed for the workshops, often arriving early for them. We also knew we had gained incredible trust from them when they shared "personal secrets" with us. One woman from CAP Nepal took much longer than the others to accept us, and she withdrew from the research midway, though we know that trust with us was not the primary reason. We know she had come to accept Sabrina as a peer and friend through some things she and her friend, another of the research participants, shared in the workshops.

Sabrina played numerous roles in the research – research assistant, interpreter, translator, transcriber, and contributor of ASRH knowledge. However, I most valued her expertise as a reproductive health education workshop facilitator as she had a very natural way of getting the women to feel at ease. Her closeness to their ages helped, but she also brought her sense of fun to the workshops, and she found ways of using non-threatening words to talk about culturally sensitive issues. For example, she called the vagina a "pipe" so the women could name it without embarrassment due to the cultural sensitivities. The conversations at the workshops were sometimes so animated, rapid, or intense, that I had to pause them to ensure I was not missing key information shared by the group. Without Sabrina, I could not have built relationships with the women. She was, in a word, indispensable to our research.

A support team of (female and male) adolescent sexual and reproductive health professionals

Another group of people who were invaluable in implementing CERM in Nepal were those familiar with ARSH issues in Nepal: Nirmala Prajapati, Saru Shilpakar, and Kamal Kafle. All had worked for the UNPFA-supported Y-PEER Nepal, and implemented ASRH education in Nepal's schools.

Nirmala helped me develop the themes of CERM (see Chapter 4). She was an early co-investigator on the project, and assisted with getting ethics approval from NHRC (See Chapter 5). She attended the pilot of CERM and provided valuable feedback on the clay body-mapping work. She also designed the "Certificates of Appreciation" to accompany gifts of doll kits we gave to the women who participated in the research (see Ong 2018). Giving certificates of appreciation is a big phenomenon in Nepal, and women find them very empowering. Saru organized the pilot of CERM and found three women over the age of 18 to participate (see Chapter 4). Kamal approached a male high school principal to plan another CERM pilot in a Kathmandu high school, though this did not advance (see Chapter 4).

Nirmala, Saru, and Kamal were remarkable ASRH advisors to the study – their knowledge on reproductive health issues from female (Nirmala and Saru) and male (Kamal) Nepali perspectives was invaluable to the shaping and implementation of CERM. They were a backbone of support for Sabrina and me.

Relationships with Asha Nepal and Centre for Awareness and Promotion Nepal

The entire CERM process could not have happened without the support of Asha Nepal and CAP Nepal, local Non-Government Organisations (NGOs) who work with sex-trafficked or sexually abused women and girls. My relationship with both began years before on other projects. By the time of our research study, a visit to the staff office at Asha Nepal was for Sabrina and I like being welcomed home. There we laughed, shared stories from the field (especially of my experiences of getting lost on my meandering walks to Asha Nepal), and drank bottomless cups of *masala chia* (Nepali spiced tea). We were included in cultural celebrations such as the Asha Nepal Christmas party and a visit to the

(Hindu) Pashpatinath temple for a *bardaman* (coming of age) ceremony for a staff member's son. It is my intention that the first launch of this book is there. *Danyabad* (thank you) for accepting us as family. Likewise, the CAP Nepal team welcomed us into their home. Sabrina and I have extremely fond memories of sitting on the rooftop in the cold while their staff and women and girls made *dhal bhat* (lentils and rice) on a *chulo* (clay stove) when gas supplies were almost non-existent during the India–Nepal border blockade (see Chapter 6). I will also always remember a Nepali word – and action – that was taught to me for use in dealing with sexual harassment by men: *jhapad* (slap). It is enacted as a forceful cheek slap. *Danyabad* Sharda Paudyal. I have come close to using it.

Conclusion

This chapter discusses the power of CERM as a time-responsive research method that enabled us to undertake data collection within a time constraint of five months. CERM has value as body-related work with populations with low literacy where traditional body-mapping methods (i.e., drawing technique) may not be successful. CERM could be well-placed for use in sexual and reproductive health education, especially with low-literate populations who understand the body experientially. In part, this can be from peer learning, which was striking in our research study. CERM has its dangers – the use of clay and photography can elicit trauma for research participants and perhaps for the researchers too. We cannot emphasize enough the importance of training in body mapping, the therapeutic use of clay and associated photography.

One of the ways we minimized the dangers of working with CERM was to ensure we had people with the right expertise on it and supporting us. We had a researcher trained in creative arts therapy and chose a young female bilingual Nepali research assistant with experience facilitating ASRH education workshops in Nepal, who was trained in the application of CERM and of the same gender and of similar age to the women we researched. It also included a support team of young women and men who had expertise in the delivery of ASRH education in Nepal. Lastly, our research study worked thanks to the strong support and close prior relationship with our partner organizations, Asha Nepal and CAP Nepal.

The next chapter offers final reflections on the book and plans for the use of CERM into the future.

References

Bennett, L.R. 2017. Indigenous healing knowledge and infertility in Indonesia: Learning about cultural safety from Sasak midwives. *Medical Anthropology*, 36(2), 111–24.

Boydell, K. et al. 2020. Applying body-mapping to research with marginalised and vulnerable groups. In: K. Boydell, ed., *Applying body-mapping in research: an arts-based method.* New York: Routledge, 6–17.

Elbrecht, C. 2012. *Trauma healing at the clay field: a sensorimotor art therapy approach.* London: Jessica Kingsley Publishers.

Harman, J., Kaufman, M. and Shrestha, D. 2014. Evaluation of the "Let's Talk" Safer Sex Intervention in Nepal. *Journal of Health Communication*, 19(8), 1–11.

Jager, A. et al. 2016. Embodied ways of storytelling the self: a systematic review of body-mapping. *Forum: Qualitative Social Research*, 17(2). http://www.qualitative-research.net/index.php/fqs/article/view/2526/3986 [Accessed 24 April 2022].

Lamichhane, P. et al. 2011. Women's status and violence against young married women in rural Nepal. *BMC Women's Health*, 1(11), 1–9.

Liamputtong, P. 2007. *Researching the vulnerable: a guide to sensitive research methods.* London: Sage.

MacCormack, C. 1985. Lay concepts affecting utilisation of family planning services in Jamaica. *Journal of Tropical Medicine and Hygiene*, 88(4), 281–5.

Ong, P. 2018. *Reproductive health for the marginalised: knowledge of young women trafficked into the sex industry in Nepal.* Thesis (PhD). Deakin University.

Ong, T., Mellor, D. and Chettri, S. 2020. Clay as a medium in three-dimensional body-mapping. *Forum Qualitative Sozialforschung/Forum: Qualitative Social Research*, 21(2), art. 9.

Orchard, T. 2017. *Remembering the body: ethical issues in body-mapping research.* New York: Springer International Publishing.

Puri, M., Shah, I. and Tamang, J. 2010. Exploring the nature and reasons for sexual violence within marriage among young women in Nepal. *Journal of Interpersonal Violence*, 25(10), 1873–92.

Puri, M., Tamang, J. and Shah, I. 2011. Suffering in silence: consequences of sexual violence within marriage among young women in Nepal. *BMC Public Health*, 11(1), 1–10. doi: 10.1186/1471-2458-11-29.

Puri, M. et al. 2012. The prevalence and determinants of sexual violence against young married women by husbands in rural Nepal. *BMC Research Notes*, 5(1), 1–13.

Regmi, P. et al. 2011. Dating and sex among emerging adults in Nepal. *Journal of Adolescent Research*, 26(6), 675–700.

Sherwood, P. 2004. *Healing art of clay therapy.* Camberwell: Australian Council for Educational Research.

Solomon, J. 2020. Foreword. In: K. Boydell, ed., *Applying body-mapping in research: an arts-based method.* New York: Routledge, xvi–xx.

8 Moving forward

Nepal and beyond

Clay Embodiment Research Method and ways of knowing

This book explores the development and use of CERM. CERM uses active observation of participants, a series of participatory-thematic clay body-mapping workshops, and group interviews centred on clay work photographs, to explore perspectives and knowledge of its participants. It is primarily underpinned by feminist research methods and feminist theory and so begins with the perspectives of stigmatized, oppressed, and marginalized women, because their world view is important. We discuss its use with young women who have been trafficked into the sex industry in Nepal, to elicit their reproductive health knowledge. Our work in Nepal showed how effective CERM is as a culturally sensitive research method for meaningfully engaging with this vulnerable – stigmatized, oppressed, and marginalized – group of women of low literacy.

CERM applies these women's ways of knowing – visually, in three dimensions (i.e., clay body-mapping), two dimensions (i.e., photography), and through audition (listening, questioning, and sharing experiences and perspectives). Clay itself is a culturally familiar material for Nepalese women. For them, traditional body-mapping methods of drawing in an outline of a human body on paper (MacCormack 1985) is likely to be an unusual form of expression. Drawing is not a commonly practised art in Nepali culture and less so in rural communities (Butcher and Kievelitz 1997, Sturley 2000) where all our women originated from (see Chapter 3). Moreover, the act of tracing around their human body (see Solomon 2007, 2020) could immediately trigger trauma in our group of women. On the other hand, while clay connects to the body, using clay does not involve a direct engagement with the body (as in Solomon's body tracing method). This gives participants the opportunity to talk about the body at a "distance" (i.e., through

DOI: 10.4324/b23275-8

clay sculptures) and facilitators have moments to anticipate the known risk of trauma elicitation in clay whilst observing participants engage in clay body-mapping. Compared with traditional methods, moreover, we found CERM to be a fast and efficient method for gathering in-depth insights into Nepalese society and culture, reproductive health issues, and the personal lives of the women and girls in our study.

There are practicalities to consider when using clay, such as messiness and temperature reactivity. Dealing with these will require prior familiarity and experience in the use of the material. However, all issues pointed out with body-mapping reinforce the importance of proper training for facilitators using CERM and especially in the therapeutic use of clay (and associated photography) (see Chapter 7).

Clay body-mapping in reproductive health education in Nepal's schools?

One promising observation from our CERM research study is that it may be a powerful tool for reproductive health education for low literacy groups. There remain uncertainties to resolve on this tract, one of which struck me after I later facilitated an incidental workshop in Nepal for 23 activists, educators, and researchers from Nepal and the United Kingdom. The aim was to share my work with the CERM via a workshop where they used clay as a medium for visualizing menstruation. It was funded by Global Action Nepal and other funding bodies associated with Dr. Sara Parker's research project on menstruation in Nepal (see Liverpool John Moores University 2021). Everyone there seemed excited by the clay and the messiness, except for a male school principal whom I noticed seemed resistant to engage with the clay. At the time, I only pondered this lightly, and nothing came up about it in our post-workshop discussions in which he was noticeably absent. Later I reflected on this: Was he doubting the value of the activity for schools? Or perhaps he was concerned about practicalities – the messiness, impacts on facilities (e.g., clay residue blocking drains), the time teachers or students (if it were a school setting) would need to devote to the cleaning up required, the care required in storing clay etc. I wondered if a reaction like this from a principal could be a barrier to introducing such clay work in, for example, Comprehensive Sexuality Education (CSE) in Nepal's school curriculum , which had been discussed many times by me and my then research assistant, Sabrina Chettri after our research study, and which we both thought was worth developing further.

There were other important uncertainties about the adaptation of CERM for reproductive health education in Nepal's schools that also need careful consideration. The most important relates to the risk of eliciting trauma for those vulnerable to it. Sexual violent is highly prevalent in Nepal and it seems reasonable to assume that some school children have been traumatized by it. (While writing this book, the case of a schoolgirl experiencing sexual abuse from a male teacher was front and centre on social media as new exposure to this issue increases in Nepal.) What if the clay work spontaneously elicited trauma? It had done so in our clay body-mapping workshops with the sex-trafficked women and girls. Who would manage this when there are unlikely to be counsellors available in Nepal's schools? It is not realistic to expect teachers or students to manage this, and it certainly should not be the case without training in trauma response. Who should be trained in the application of clay body mapping workshops in educational settings? In Nepal, there have already been barriers (i.e., with teachers and parents) to implementing reproductive health education in schools due to the cultural sensitivity of the topic. However, we have since identified potential opportunities for training through, for example, the UNPFA-supported Youth Peer Nepal (Y-PEER Nepal) who are actively engaged in initiatives in ASRH education in Nepal's schools. Then, of course, funding is a perennial challenge. We clearly have much to work through if CERM is to someday contribute to improved reproductive health education in Nepal, especially in schools.

Further steps

Clay body-mapping is fun, fast, and dangerous. CERM captures this in a structured form for reproductive health research. The method also has great promise as an education tool. Our work and journal papers on CERM and its use in Nepal (see Ong 2018, Ong, Mellor and Chettri 2019. 2020, 2021) is attracting interest. I have been asked about how one goes about applying it in various contexts and for purposes quite different from our use of it with stigmatized, oppressed, and marginalized Nepalese sex-trafficked women with low literacy. I have come across descriptions of research projects that seem to have used clay, but without the knowledge of trauma elicitation. Indeed, the prime reason for writing this book is, in response, to provide researchers, educators, and therapists an insight into how we went about designing a research method for sensitive research with vulnerable populations in another culture. Our hope is that it provides a basis for thoughtful reflection on ways to meaningfully connect with people in other cultures. It would be brilliant if this leads to its further development, and the application of CERM in diverse fields with considered care.

But even before this book took shape, I realized from the early interest in our work that the competencies required for the effective and safe use of CERM may not be well recognized and appreciated, or can be made readily available by us and other early users. So, with Sabrina Chettri, my research assistant in Nepal, we hope to develop a CERM training manual that is trauma informed as well as covers managing other key risks (i.e., Covid-19 and silica in clay dust). It may be that we also return to the field of creative arts therapy to help us develop a specialized training programme as training should not be given a "light touch".

Call to action

Still, the development and use of CERM is in an early phase. More research into its use, and the use of clay in research methods generally, will make it more robust, particularly in the reproductive health field with low-literate, vulnerable, stigmatized, oppressed, and marginalized populations in cultures where such topics are extremely sensitive. Good research will grow the beautiful work we began in Nepal.

References

Butcher, K. and Kievelitz, U. 1997. Planning with PRA: HIV and STD in a Nepalese mountain community. *Health and Policy Planning*, 12(3), 253–61.

Liverpool John Moores University. 2021. *Dignity without danger: collaboratively analysing stigma and taboos to develop innovative strategies to address menstrual exclusion in Nepal*. Liverpool: Liverpool John Moores University. www.ljmu.ac.uk/microsites/dignity-without-danger/ [Accessed 8 May 2022].

MacCormack, C. 1985. Lay concepts affecting utilisation of family planning services in Jamaica. *Journal of Tropical Medicine and Hygiene*, 88(4), 281–5.

Ong T., Mellor, D. and Chettri, S. 2019. Multiplicity of stigma: the experiences, fears and knowledge of young trafficked women in Nepal. *Sexual and Reproductive health Matters*, 27(3), 32–48.

Ong, T., Mellor, D. and Chettri, S. 2020. Clay as a medium in three-dimensional body-mapping. *Forum: Qualitative Social Research*, 21(2), art. 9. https://www.qualitative-research.net/index.php/fqs/article/download/3380/4567?inline=1 [Accessed 12 March 2022].

Ong, T., Mellor, D. and Chettri, S. 2021. "Females are always dominated and disregarded by males, just because they are female": the continuation of patriarchal norms for young trafficked women in Nepal. *Culture, Health and Sexuality*, 1–16.

Ong, P. 2018. *Reproductive health for the marginalised: knowledge of young women trafficked into the sex industry in Nepal*. Thesis (PhD). Deakin University.

Solomon, J. 2007. *Living with X: A body-mapping journey in the time of HIV/AIDS: a facilitator's guide.* Johannesburg: Regional Psychosocial Support Initiative.

Solomon, J. 2020. Foreword. In: K. Boydell, ed., *Applying body-mapping in research: an arts-based method.* New York: Routledge, xvi–xx.

Sturley, A. 2000. *Mapping the effects of vasectomy.*, *PLA Note 37: Special Issue: Sexual and Reproductive Health.* Holborn: International Institute for Environment and Development, 17, 83–6. http://pubs.iied.org/pdfs/6335I IED.pdf [Accessed 21 April 2022].

Index

For Product Safety Concerns and Information please contact our EU
representative GPSR@taylorandfrancis.com
Taylor & Francis Verlag GmbH, Kaufingerstraße 24, 80331 München, Germany